MW00611996

LIVING A DEEPLY INSIGHTFUL LIFE

Living a Deeply Insightful Life

Based on

RAV NOACH WEINBERG'S 48 WAYS

by

Rabbi Chaim Willis

KTAV PUBLISHING

URIM PUBLICATIONS
Jerusalem · New York

Living A Deeply Insightful Life
Based on Rav Noach Weinberg's 48 Ways

By Rabbi Chaim Willis

Typeset by Ariel Walden

Printed in Israel

First Edition

ISBN: 978-1-60280-395-4

KTAV Publishing
527 Empire Boulevard
Brooklyn, NY 11225
www.ktav.com

Urim Publications
P.O. Box 52287,
Jerusalem 9152102
Israel
www.UrimPublications.com

Library of Congress Cataloging-in-Publication Data in progress.

Rabbi Yitzchak Berkovits
Sanhedria HaMurchevet 113/27
Jerusalem, Israel 97707
02-5813847

יצחק שמואל הלוי ברקוביץ
ראש רשת כוללים לינת הצדק
סנהדרי״ה המורחבת 113/27
ירושלם ת״ו

בס״ד ירושלים ת״ו כ״ז אדר ב' תשע״ט

Rabbi Chaim Willis is one of the most brilliant human beings I know. I will not forget his insightful input in my early days of teaching at Aish HaTorah, and I consider him a mentor in my understanding of the mindset of the adult beginner in Torah.

Rav Noach Weinberg zt"l's 48 Ways to Wisdom is a comprehensive guide to mastering Torah and Life in general. Rabbi Willis, as one of Rav Noach's closest students, absorbed every word and made it his life. I am confident this rendition of the 48 Ways will serve to change the lives of all those who read it, observant or non-observant, young and old.

May HaShem grant Rabbi Willis the opportunity to reach the masses with his profundity and wisdom for years to come.

בברכה,

יצחק ברקוביץ

Contents

Contents

Dedication

This book is dedicated to the memory of my teacher Rabbi Noach Weinberg *z"tl*. His commitment to the Almighty's cause and to the Jewish people, his deep wisdom and his concern for Jews, led to tens of thousands of Jews coming back to their people, me among them. May his wisdom and example continue to lead the Jewish people back to their destiny.

Acknowledgements

I have wanted to write a book on the 48 Ways for many years, but I didn't get around to it until I was helped and pushed by my friend Tuvia Frame. Thanks Tuvia for your belief in the potential of the book and your help in getting it published.

Solly Krok is one of the legends of Jewish Johannesburg. Jewish outreach in South Africa, including Aish Hatorah in Johannesburg, was only made possible through his support. Thanks Solly for your help in the past and for your help in getting this book published. May it be a belated gift for your 90th birthday!

Thanks to all those who helped in sponsoring this book:

Ashley Cohen	Dr. Gordon Kretzmer
Simcha Diskin	Solly Krok
David Esra	Shaun Matisson
Justin Fishpen	Renney Plit
Daniel Ginsburg	Roland Sassoon
Moshe Immerman	Dr. Michael Setzer
	Jake Willis

May we all continue to work together to help the Jewish people.

Thanks to all my colleagues and staff at Aish Hatorah South Africa in Johannesburg who keep alive the fire of Torah that Rabbi Weinberg started in Jerusalem 45 years ago.

Thanks and love to my wife Shelley and all my children, who give me all their love and support in teaching and writing.

And most of all, thanks to the Almighty, the real source of all our wisdom and accomplishments.

Introduction

I first came in contact with Rabbi Noach Weinberg and Aish Hatorah in Jerusalem in 1975. I was a secular young man, 24 years old, from a left-wing Jewish family in New York, finishing a year-long trip backpacking through Asia. Although my family was Jewish, it didn't mean anything to me. If anyone would have asked me whether I believed in G-d, I would have said "no" or "I don't know." Certainly nothing like a G-d who gave a Torah to the Jews.

Aish Hatorah changed that, and the key to that change was Rabbi Noach Weinberg and his class on the 48 Ways. Rav Noach was charismatic, and his class was a great show. But it had deep ideas interspersed among the catchy slogans. "What is the opposite of pain? Pleasure? No, it's comfort." "Can you be commanded to love? Only if you have a definition of love." "Clarity or death." "A fool learns from his own mistakes, a wise man learns from the mistakes of others." "If you ask a good man or an evil man are you a good man, who is more likely to say that he is a good man?" "If you don't know what you are living for, you're a walking donkey."

The class changed my perceptions and the perceptions of many like me. Many of us moved on from the 48 Ways to what we considered the core aspects of Judaism – mitzvot, Jewish law, Talmud and other textual Torah learning.

What we didn't realize at the time was how deep and comprehensive the ideas of the 48 Ways were. Beginners in Judaism, not yet even convinced we believed in G-d and Torah, we could only appreciate the ideas on a beginning level. And those ideas were only a part of the "show" that was necessary to engage and motivate us to go further with our exploration of Judaism.

Yet Rav Noach never considered that the 48 Ways was material for beginners. He looked at it as fundamental ideas about life that every Jew needed to know. He felt he was teaching over the deep understanding about how to acquire Torah that the Sages of the Mishna had listed in short and concise phrases, each one with great meaning. Although he used it as a vehicle to attract beginners, he thought that its wisdom was crucial for anyone in the Torah world, including those who had learned in yeshivot for years.

Because it was given as a class for beginners – with all the necessary simplification and dramatization that this entailed – the full value of the 48 Ways has never been fully appreciated, even by those who learned them directly from Rav Noach.

It is the goal of this book to demonstrate some of the real depth of the 48 Ways. I have tried to explain Rav Noach's understanding of the Sages in a way that any person, including knowledgeable and observant Jews, can appreciate.

The ideas dealt with in the 48 Ways are relevant to all of us. Why is learning Torah so crucial to personal development? What is intuition? How do we handle the struggle between the body and the soul? How do we understand ourselves? How do we control emotions, fight negative ones and develop the right ones? How do we use the physical world positively? What are the definitions of concepts we know we should live with – humbleness, joy, love – and how do those definitions help us to achieve them? How can we work to understand and help others to deal with their problems? What is greatness and how do we work to achieve it? All this and more is in the 48 Ways, with practical suggestions on how to use these ideas in living.

In writing this book on the 48 Ways, I have started from a complete set of notes I took more than 40 years ago. Temporarily drained from study of Talmud, I took time off to revisit Rav Noach's beginner's class on the 48 Ways. Having spent some time in yeshiva, I could appreciate much more about it than I did when I first started at Aish. I saw that it was a comprehensive and deep presentation of necessary Jewish ideas about living, not just something for beginners. I have been teaching it to people on many different levels ever since.

In this book, I haven't tried to imitate Rav Noach's style. I have reorganized the structure of many of the Ways, using a more analytical and less intuitive style than Rav Noach's classes. And I have added explanations and examples that I have heard from others or that I have used in my years of teaching. But I have tried to be faithful to the core of Rav Noach's wisdom, which he considered to be not his own, but his understanding of what the Sages were explaining in their catalogue of the 48 Ways.

I hope this book will serve as a clear, organized and easily understandable presentation of a set of ideas that has already changed the world of many returnees to Judaism, but still has great relevance to the larger Jewish world.

Text of the 48 Ways[1]

גְּדוֹלָה תוֹרָה יוֹתֵר מִן הַכְּהוּנָה וּמִן הַמַּלְכוּת, שֶׁהַמַּלְכוּת נִקְנֵית בִּשְׁלֹשִׁים מַעֲלוֹת, וְהַכְּהֻנָּה בְּעֶשְׂרִים וְאַרְבַּע, וְהַתּוֹרָה נִקְנֵית בְּאַרְבָּעִים וּשְׁמוֹנָה דְבָרִים, וְאֵלּוּ הֵן:

בְּתַלְמוּד, בִּשְׁמִיעַת הָאֹזֶן, בַּעֲרִיכַת שְׂפָתַיִם, בְּבִינַת הַלֵּב, בְּאֵימָה, בְּיִרְאָה, בַּעֲנָוָה, בְּשִׂמְחָה, בְּטָהֳרָה, בְּשִׁמּוּשׁ חֲכָמִים, בְּדִקְדּוּק חֲבֵרִים, בְּפִלְפּוּל הַתַּלְמִידִים, בְּיִשּׁוּב, בְּמִקְרָא, בְּמִשְׁנָה, בְּמִעוּט סְחוֹרָה, בְּמִעוּט דֶּרֶךְ אֶרֶץ, בְּמִעוּט תַּעֲנוּג, בְּמִעוּט שֵׁנָה, בְּמִעוּט שִׂיחָה, בְּמִעוּט שְׂחוֹק, בְּאֶרֶךְ אַפַּיִם, בְּלֵב טוֹב, בֶּאֱמוּנַת חֲכָמִים, בְּקַבָּלַת הַיִּסּוּרִין, הַמַּכִּיר אֶת מְקוֹמוֹ, וְהַשָּׂמֵחַ בְּחֶלְקוֹ, וְהָעוֹשֶׂה סְיָג לִדְבָרָיו, וְאֵינוֹ מַחֲזִיק טוֹבָה לְעַצְמוֹ, אָהוּב, אוֹהֵב אֶת הַמָּקוֹם, אוֹהֵב אֶת הַבְּרִיּוֹת, אוֹהֵב אֶת הַצְּדָקוֹת, אוֹהֵב אֶת הַמֵּישָׁרִים, אוֹהֵב אֶת הַתּוֹכָחוֹת, וּמִתְרַחֵק מִן הַכָּבוֹד, וְלֹא מֵגִיס לִבּוֹ בְּתַלְמוּדוֹ, וְאֵינוֹ שָׂמֵחַ בְּהוֹרָאָה, נוֹשֵׂא בְעֹל עִם חֲבֵרוֹ, וּמַכְרִיעוֹ לְכַף זְכוּת, וּמַעֲמִידוֹ עַל הָאֱמֶת, וּמַעֲמִידוֹ עַל הַשָּׁלוֹם, וּמִתְיַשֵּׁב לִבּוֹ בְּתַלְמוּדוֹ, שׁוֹאֵל וּמֵשִׁיב שׁוֹמֵעַ וּמוֹסִיף, הַלּוֹמֵד עַל מְנָת לְלַמֵּד וְהַלּוֹמֵד עַל מְנָת לַעֲשׂוֹת, הַמַּחְכִּים אֶת רַבּוֹ, וְהַמְכַוֵּן אֶת שְׁמוּעָתוֹ, וְהָאוֹמֵר דָּבָר בְּשֵׁם אוֹמְרוֹ, הָא לָמַדְתָּ כָּל הָאוֹמֵר דָּבָר בְּשֵׁם אוֹמְרוֹ מֵבִיא גְאֻלָּה לָעוֹלָם, שֶׁנֶּאֱמַר וַתֹּאמֶר אֶסְתֵּר לַמֶּלֶךְ בְּשֵׁם מָרְדֳּכָי:

Torah is even greater than the priesthood or royalty, for royalty is acquired with 30 benefits, and the priesthood is acquired with twenty-four, but Torah is acquired through 48 Ways, which are:

---

1. Following is the source text of the 48 Ways in Hebrew and in English. The 48 Ways is from a collection of rabbinic statements called *Masechta Kallah Rabbati*. It is often learned as part of Pirke Avos, and is included in *siddurim* as part of the sixth chapter of Pirke Avos, Mishne 6. The English translation is my own, and follows the idea of the Way, rather than the literal translation. In my book, I explain some of the insights that come from a more literal translation of the Hebrew text.

Study, listening, speaking it out on the lips, the understanding of the heart, awe, fear, humility, joy, purity, serving wise men, careful analysis with friends, the questioning of students, deliberateness, the Written Law, the Oral Law, minimize business, minimize derech eretz, minimize physical pleasure, minimize sleep, minimize conversation, minimize laughter, being slow to anger, having a good heart, believing in wise men, accepting pain, recognizing one's place, being happy with one's portion, making a fence for one's things, not considering yourself special, being beloved, loving 'the Place', loving the creations, loving doing the right things, loving the straight path, loving criticism, keeping far from honor, not becoming bored in one's learning, not taking joy in teaching others what to do, sharing the burden with your fellow man, motivating him to go in the right direction, giving him true clarity, giving him inner peace, becoming absorbed in one's study, asking and answering, hearing and adding on, learning in order to teach, learning in order to do, making one's teacher wise, directing one's learning, saying something in the name of the one who said it.

Behold, you have learned: Anyone who says something in the name of the one who said it brings redemption to the world, as it says: "Esther said to the king in the name of Mordechai."[2]

---

2. See Bringing the World to Redemption in Way #50.

Way · 1

Life-Long Study

⸶ How we live is based on what we think.

⸶ Knowing about how to live is based on the accuracy and truthfulness of the information that we have.

⸶ G-d's Torah is "Torat Chaim," "Instructions for Living." It contains all the information we need to make decisions in life.

⸶ Our ability to make productive decisions is based on how much Torah we have learned.

⸶ Personal growth requires a life-long intensive search for greater knowledge, in order to give us the basis to make meaningful and productive decisions.

The first of the 48 Ways to acquiring wisdom is *B'Talmud*, "with study." That seems reasonable enough – how would you otherwise acquire wisdom without studying it?

But the Sages included methodologies of study in Ways #43–49. *B'Talmud*, the first of the Ways, is referring to the *commitment* to study as the foundation for acquiring wisdom.

This commitment to study is the core of Judaism, and is unique among all world religions and philosophies. While Islam, Christianity and Hinduism each include some religious study, and the secular world has its share of philosophers and researchers, none of them emphasize study to the extent that Judaism does, requiring every person – rich, poor, healthy, or sick – to study every day, for their entire lives. None of them calls for the acquisition of such a vast amount of information on every subject, so much so that Rabbi Tarfon, in Pirke Avos, needs to tell us regarding learning Torah "it isn't upon us to finish the work, but we aren't free to waste time from it."

A commitment to study to such an extent requires an explanation. Why is study so central to Judaism?

The answer to that question lies in the very nature of human beings and our purpose in the world. As explained by many of the great philosophical texts of Judaism, a human being is a spiritual soul placed in a physical body. The soul is driven to connect with the spiritual, to achieve meaning, to be good, to love G-d and other human beings. The body is driven by physical comfort and gratification (see Way #4 – "Connecting with Your Intuition: Understanding of the Heart," where we share techniques for identifying the soul-body conflict in all of us). The purpose of life is for the soul to use its power of free will to control the body and turn the whole human being, body and soul, towards spiritual goals.

When placed in the body, the soul loses the direct awareness it has when it is outside the body. It can't directly control the body. It needs to use an intermediate entity, the mind.

The mind is a machine much like a computer, storing and processing information about life. When we access the mind, it gives us the information we are searching for. Based on that information, we make decisions. (See Ways #4, 44–49 for more on this topic.)

Every conscious act we do as human beings is a result of what our minds tell us. What we believe – whether there is a G-d or there isn't, what we think is good and not good, what we choose as a profession, who we choose to marry and if we choose to marry – all stem from what we think. If the mind has acquired accurate information, the soul can use it to choose the beliefs and actions that will help us grow and succeed in life. We call that ability of the soul the *yetzer hatov*, "the good inclination." If the mind is lacking information, or if it picks up mistaken or even harmful ideas that inundate today's society, the body can use that misleading information to confuse the soul about what is true and meaningful. This ability of the body is often referred to as the *yetzer hara*, "the evil inclination."

My teacher Rabbi Noach Weinberg used to say "the battle for life is the battle for sanity." Everything depends on the soul's ability to get the mind working on its behalf in opposition to the body's effort to get the mind on its side.

To help us succeed in this conflict, the Almighty gave us Torah. We call our Torah, *Torat Chaim*, "Instructions for Living." It is a vast compendium of all the information we need to know about living – what life is about, what is real pleasure, what is good and what is meaningful, and what are the actions we need to take in life to successfully achieve our goals. It has multiple levels of depth, so much so that one of Job's wise friends said, "Its measure is longer than the earth and wider than the sea."

In order to master and use this vast knowledge, we have to start by recognizing how important it is to have it. Then we can accept the commitment to what is involved in acquiring it.

FIVE COMMITMENTS TO LEARNING

In teaching this Way, Rabbi Weinberg listed five commitments we need to make in order to fully maximize our potential to acquire this knowledge: Constant, Consistent, Continuous, Repetitive, and Making it an Identity. All of them are based on what is necessary to make the best use of our minds.

Constant. The amount of information we need to know for living is very extensive. The Talmud, the central text of the Oral Law that is the foundation of Jewish law, takes seven years to learn at a pace of one page a day. That page may take you one to two hours a day to learn, even on a superficial level, without commentaries and deeper understanding. That doesn't include the Five Books of the Written Torah, or the books of the Prophets or the other books of Tanach such as Job and Koheles and Daniel. In addition, there is a vast collection of great Jewish books of philosophy and personal growth. Beyond that there is the Kabbalistic tradition.

As mentioned, Rabbi Tarfon teaches us that the study of Torah is a never-ending task. Even a person with the whole day available to learn, will never complete the study of the entire Torah. If you have only one hour a day to learn, how much of it will you be able to do?

The good news is that we all have much more time to use for learning than we realize. When you are having breakfast, read a book of Torah wisdom or think about some issue that came up in your learning previously. When you are driving to work, put on a Torah CD. What can you learn or think about during coffee breaks or at lunch time? Is there something you can learn while at the gym instead of listening to music? When you get home, talk to your spouse and children, but spend less time checking out the news or Facebook. Use Way #19 – "Minimize Sleep," discussed later, to add some learning time before you go to sleep.

To use all your time effectively, you need a plan. What aspects of the Torah do you want to learn, and how can you incorporate it into your day? Today there are many books in English, Torah talks on CDs or on YouTube on any conceivable topic. Fill in those spare moments of your day with what is right for you and in the most efficient way you can access them. Even though you won't know it all, there is much to gain from whatever additional knowledge you acquire. Time is life itself, so don't waste it.

The Sages also said to be **consistent**. Set a time for learning, the same time every day. A person who has a set time to go to the gym every day will follow a routine easily. If every day he has to decide when and if to go, his natural laziness will fight against him doing it. Even more so with learning, which is a tough exercise for the mind, and requires discipline and commitment. By setting a set time for learning, it becomes a habit, and is much easier to stick with.

Continuous learning is the way to get deeper insights into Torah. The mind is a machine, and when it rests, it is difficult to start it up again. Once it is moving, it is easier to keep it moving. When you are learning continuously for a few hours, your mind finds it easier to connect with other information in your mind to understand something in a deeper way. When you interrupt to get a cup of coffee or look at your cell phone, the process has to start again from the beginning.

The great Torah Sage Maimonides said that the majority of a person's wisdom comes from learning at night. Why? Because (especially in Talmudic days, before electric lights), when everyone else was asleep and there were no interruptions, the Torah scholar, learning alone by candlelight, would have nothing to block him from reaching deeper levels of wisdom. Today, when no time is free of distractions, we need to make a special effort to create space for ourselves for thinking more deeply about life.

Learning something once is not enough. Learning needs to be

repetitive. For our wisdom to be effective and applicable in everyday living, it must be in the forefront of our minds. We often don't remember something the first time. Even if we do, we tend to forget it over time. For knowledge to be truly incorporated into our brain, we have to review it enough times so that it is ingrained in our memory.

In addition, remembering doesn't necessarily mean understanding. By returning to a subject that we learned previously in our lives, we are able to add to it all the information we have learned since, and all the deeper insights we have picked up by our personal growth over time.

Finally, being a learner needs to be an *identity*. In Western society, the answer to the question "what do you do" is to state your profession. However, it should be: I am a thinker, a philosopher. My commitment is to understand what life is about and how to make the most out of it.

Way · 2

Listening to Life's Messages

¶ The first step to achieving wisdom is to learn to listen to the wisdom that G-d is constantly sending us.

¶ Wisdom can come from people, it can come from events, and it can come from Torah.

¶ In order to acquire wisdom, it must be heard, analyzed, and then examined for its deeper meaning.

¶ To listen effectively to that wisdom, learn to ask the question: "What?"

¶ The most significant "What?" question to ask is: What am I living for? What is the purpose of life?

The Hebrew term for Way #2 of the 48 Ways is *B'Shmiat HaOzen*, "listening." Listening comes right after Way #1 – Life-Long Study, because the people and the world around us are our first and greatest source of wisdom (even the Torah we learn has to come from those teaching us).

The Mishna teaches that a person should always say "the world was created for *me*." An all-powerful G-d does not need to economize on space or effort. He could easily create a whole world for any of us, individually. The only reason other people and everything else are in your world is because it benefits you. And that benefit can't be only physical – even a billionaire can only experience a small part of the world's physical pleasures.

"The world is created for me" means that G-d created everything in the world to teach *me*. Every human being, every natural phenomenon, every event, has lessons about life that can be discovered. To develop ourselves, we must learn to "listen" to those lessons.

The first and most necessary place to seek wisdom is from other people. The insights and experiences of others are one of the most important ways G-d communicates with us. We can't access that wisdom unless we learn to listen to people.

This is not always easy for us. It takes effort to listen to someone, and often we don't have the energy to make that effort. However, that isn't the only reason we don't listen. We may be distracted by our own problems so we don't focus on what someone else is saying. If we don't respect a person enough, we are likely not to make the effort to hear him or her out. Even if the person is a respected rabbi or our spouse whom we love and respect, we might not want to hear what he or she has to say, in case it might involve having to change our ways.

So the first step to listening is to be willing to make the effort to pay attention. Just as we have the ability to control our arms and legs, we also have the ability to control our minds. If someone is speaking to you, make a conscious decision to listen.

That's the first step, but it isn't enough. It is necessary to make the effort to summarize and evaluate what you hear. Sometimes people express themselves with words or thoughts that are valid and logical, while other times they may be misinformed. Even if what they say is true, they may not always express it well. The key to evaluating what you hear is to ask the question: what is being said?

When someone says something on an important subject, always ask yourself: what did he or she say? When your rabbi speaks in the synagogue for 30 minutes, ask yourself: what is he saying? Do I agree or not? When your spouse has a complaint about what you did, ask yourself: what is the exact complaint? Then decide: Is he/she right or wrong? What should I do about it?

But that *still* isn't enough. You also have to learn to ask: what did the person mean by what was said? Words are frequently used which have more than one interpretation or definition. Often they are used incorrectly.

Rabbi Noach Weinberg used to share a story that illustrates the confusion caused by words used without definitions.

In the early days of Aish Hatorah, Rabbi Meir Shuster, *zt"l*, would bring young adults from the Western Wall to the yeshiva (I was among those fortunate ones, many years ago). Rabbi Noach Weinberg would engage them in conversation. He would encourage them to pursue their Jewishness through studying for a short time at Aish. A young man came into his office (so the story goes), and told him: "Rabbi, I don't need to discuss G-d with you, I am an atheist." Rav Noach answered: "An atheist, that's great! I always wanted to meet an atheist! An atheist (Rav Noach gives a definition) is someone who knows there is no G-d. To "know," you must have evidence. Please, tell me what it is!"

The young man had no evidence. Much like the average youth in western society, he hadn't really considered the issue. So he replied: "What I meant to say is that I am an agnostic."

Rav Noach continued: "An agnostic, that's great also! An agnostic (another definition) is someone who *knows* that it is impossible to *know* whether there is G-d. To *know* that, you must have evidence. Please, tell me what it is!"

The young man hadn't thought about that one either. He was forced to admit: "What I meant was, I don't know whether there is a G-d."

Rav Noach would say: "You don't know? We have evidence, come in and let us teach you."

The point of the story is more than the fact that young people today think very little about the question of G-d's existence. An even deeper point is that the young man glosses over his lack of knowledge, even to himself, by misusing words. When he says he is an atheist, he feels he has a position: you are a rabbi, I'm an atheist. You have your views, I have mine. When he realizes he just doesn't know, he can decide whether he is willing to take the time to listen.

In addition, the person listening to the "atheist" may get confused by the misuse of terms. He may think he is dealing with someone with a well thought-out philosophy, and be afraid to challenge him. Or that he is possibly a major source for wisdom on an important life issue.

Always ask people to define their understanding of terms when they argue politics or religion: what do you mean by "left-wing" or "right-wing" or "racist" or "fanatic" or "brainwashed" or "fundamentalist"? Even more so when discussing ideas about life: what do you mean by "love," or "good" or "happiness"? Later in the 48 Ways, we will give definitions for these and many other crucial ideas.

However, even this step of clarifying terms and words isn't enough to achieve what it means to really listen. Seek to understand the essence of what you hear, the central point that is being communicated.

If you just read a novel, ask yourself: what was its message? Did you learn something new? If not, maybe it wasn't worth your time.

What was the message of the movie you just saw now? Do you agree with it? Would you be happy if your kids thought that the characters in the movie were role models?

When you learn something in Torah, don't be satisfied just to understand the words or the story. Ask: what did it teach me about life? What is the message of the story about Adam and Eve and the first sin? What is the message of the story of the Flood? The Torah comes to teach us about life, not about history, and we need to ask what that teaching is.

The most significant "what" question to ask is: What am I living for? What is the purpose of life? Is it helping people, raising children, having fun, doing good deeds, or connecting with the "Ultimate Reality" behind everything? Take life, and look for the essence of it.

The Talmud says that listening to G-d (and here it means listening to the essence of what G-d is telling us) is the key to bringing the final redemption.

> Rabbi Yehoshua ben Levi asked Eliyahu the prophet: When will the *Mashiach* come? [Eliyahu] said: Go and ask him yourself! . . . [Rabbi Yehoshua goes to see the *Mashiach*] He asked him: When will you come, Master? He answered: Today. [When he returned to Eliyahu, Rabbi Yehoshua said to him] "He lied to me, for he said he would come, but he did not. Eliyahu answered: [You didn't understand him] "This is what he said to you: Today – if you will listen to G-d's voice."

May we all learn to listen to what the Almighty wants to tell us.

Way · 3

Using the Power of Speech

¶ Speech is the means by which intangible thoughts become tangible reality.

¶ By writing down our thoughts, we can look at them objectively, remember and evaluate them.

¶ Speaking out our thoughts is even more effective, because it helps us understand our emotions and how they may be impacting us.

¶ Speaking in a clear and organized way rids you of confusion and allows you to direct your words to influence others.

¶ A great speaker can influence people for good in the same way that a demagogue can use speech to influence the masses for evil.

The Hebrew term for Way #3 of the 48 Ways is *"Arichat Sfatayim,"* literally "arranging it on your lips." It deals with the importance of using the power of speech to gain wisdom.

Speech is a very central part of Judaism. Jews talk a lot, even when they shouldn't (like during prayer). A house of study, in contrast to a library, is a very noisy place.

The reason for the importance of speech is that speech is the first interface between the inner you, what you are thinking and feeling, and the outside world. It is the first public, objective sign of who you are and what you take seriously. We change our minds all the time, but when something is spoken it becomes part of the reality of the world outside. We and others can judge it, analyze it, and make commitments to live by it. That is why someone getting married has to state out loud, in words, what he is resolved to do before giving the ring, and it is why a vow – to have any consequences – needs to be spoken out.

Since the primary purpose of speech is to bring out into the world what is in your mind, the first aspect of using this tool for wisdom doesn't even require the voice at all. Even writing down what you are thinking makes it a reality in the world, and you can use a pen and paper to get clarity on important issues.

When you are going to a class or presentation on ideas, law or business, take notes! As long as information is only going into your mind, it can get lost there. By the end of the class, you can't remember most of what you heard. If you write down notes, you give the information a real existence. You can review it, examine it, and evaluate it.

When dealing with an important issue, write down pros and cons. Should you change your job? Your emotions may push your thoughts one way or the other. When you have a list in front of you of pros and cons, you can decide in a much clearer and more organized way.

Oftentimes we thought that we were going to change when we heard something that was particularly inspiring, and then we quickly forgot about it. Or we made decisions on Yom Kippur to act differently, and then we lost track of them. So write down the new idea, or sit down right after Yom Kippur and write down your decisions. Record them in a book you can go back to.

While writing down thoughts certainly helps, speaking is a much more powerful tool. Your voice is a more direct reflection of who you are. It adds emotion to the idea – how you really feel about it will come through in your voice. If you speak out a resolution, it makes it more likely that you will keep it. We have more of a sense that we have to live with what we say than with what we think.

When you think you have made a decision, saying it out loud will allow you to check – do I really mean it, am I going to carry through on it?

When you make a decision to do something that is difficult for you, talk yourself into it. Say a few times with conviction "I am going to go in and ask for a raise," and you will see that you have the power to do it.

In praying and in the service of G-d, we use this power many times a day. When we wake up we say *Modeh Ani*, thanking G-d that He has returned our soul to us for another day. We use our voice to help us feel that it is great to be alive! Before we do a mitzvah, we say out loud "Now I am preparing to do this mitzvah." We use the power of the voice to focus our attention on what we are about to do. At least two times a day, we say the *Shema* out loud, to appreciate emotionally as well as in our minds that G-d is the only real source of everything.

The most advanced use of the power of speech is indicated by the very name of this Way, "Arranging it on your lips." Say what you mean to say in as clear a way as possible without extra words. Words lose their power if they are overused or used in an unclear way. We all know what it is like to listen to a disorganized speaker who doesn't get to the point. So before you give a presentation — write it out, edit it to make it clear, and speak it out to yourself or someone else.

The Rabbis say: "Always teach your students in a minimum of words."

No less an expert on the power of words, than Adolf Hitler wrote in "Mein Kampf" that the only way to change the world was through using the power of speech. He demonstrated later how effectively he could use words to get Germans to follow him in his evil path of devastating destruction.

A Jewish understanding is that anything that can be used for evil can be used even more effectively to do good deeds. Rav Shach, the leader of yeshiva-world Jewry towards the end of the 20th century once said, "If one man can kill six million Jews, one man can save six million Jews." May we learn to use the power of speech for good with the same intensity that Hitler had when speaking for evil.

Way · 4

Connecting with your Intuition:
Understanding of the Heart

❡ According to our Sages, we are born with an inner knowledge of what life is about, and all the information necessary to lead a good and productive life.

❡ When we connect with this information, we experience an emotion of recognition. This is called "binat halev," "the understanding of the heart." It can also be referred to as "connecting with your intuition."

❡ Since our mind contains true information and false information, we must use binat halev to distinguish between the two.

❡ The more Torah information we have, the more accurate will be our ability to use our binat halev to do this.

❡ Self-understanding through introspection is one of the most important functions of binat halev.

In Way #1, *Life-Long Study*, we said that the mind is like a computer. It stores the information we need to make decisions about life. That information can come from education, especially Torah education, and from experience. Our Sages tell us that this information from education and experience is merely a reawakening of a much vaster store of information that we have from birth.

In the Talmud, our Sages described this in a powerful metaphor. When a baby is in its mother's womb, an angel teaches it all of Torah

– all the knowledge a person needs to know about living. When we are born, we lose our connection to it. However, this knowledge is not actually lost. It is stored in the "computer" of our mind. Through education, experience and introspection we rediscover and reconnect with what we were taught.

This idea is the source of the Jewish understanding that every human being can discover truth, even when the rest of the world thinks differently. It is the reason why Abraham, the ancestor of the Jewish people, could come to the conclusion that there was one G-d in a world where everyone was convinced of the truth of idol worship. It is the reason why, even today, we can identify and live with the Torah ideas that we learn, even when most of the world disagrees with them.

But if we have an inner understanding of truth, why is there so much falsehood in the world? Why do so many people disagree over so many fundamental things?

The reason is that getting in touch with the inner understanding is not easy. Our mind absorbs a range of information from mistaken ideas of confused societies, questionable education and bad experiences. These ideas become stuck in the mind like computer viruses, and short-circuit our ability to get in touch with the true ideas we were taught by the angel.

So how do we know, when we learn something or think about an idea, that this is the Torah that we were taught and not a false idea planted in the mind?

As we mentioned in Way #1, having a true outside source of information – G-d's Torah which was given at Mount Sinai – helps us connect with what we were taught. And that information enables us to judge new information that we receive from other sources.

But learning about life is a 24/7 experience, and we are constantly picking up information from our environment and from other people. How do we judge when that information is true or not true?

The key to doing this is Way #4 – "Connecting with Your Intuition: Understanding of the Heart." When we hear a true idea, we feel an emotion of recognition. This emotion is the soul's way of validating an idea. It is called "the understanding of the heart," because, in Judaism (as in the Western world), the heart is considered the source of emotions.

Sometimes validating an idea is easy. In many years of teaching non-observant students, I have seen that most will have no trouble agreeing with the idea that *loshen hora*, speaking badly about others, is wrong, even when the negative information that the speaker is saying is true. They recognize the truth of this despite the fact that they have never heard the idea before, and despite the fact that a good part of their social interactions are based on speaking badly about others.

So how did they know it was right? Their capacity of *Binat Halev* picked up that it was a true idea, even though it was ignored by their society.

Not every idea is as easy to connect with. Our physical desires prevent us from connecting with what we know. Try telling a secular young man today that pre-marital sex is wrong. Out come the "computer viruses" – the wrong ideas they have learned: it is religious fanaticism to think that, religion doesn't like you to have fun, everybody does it so what could be wrong with it, it's two consenting adults, how would you know who to marry otherwise, etc.

Ask him what arguments he can come up with for it being wrong. For the normal secular guy, the mind shuts down and he can't think of any. If you ask him to reflect and find in himself the intuition that it is wrong (as was the general consensus of all Western society, Jewish, Christian, and Muslim, until a few years ago), he won't be able to. His body doesn't want to let him go there.

The Rabbis explained this process long ago. They said that when a person does something wrong, he is bothered by it. When he repeats it, it becomes permissible to him. He loses touch with his inner knowledge of truth.

Most ideas are somewhere in between. The more information you have, the more you can hone in on what is true and what is the right course of action. But you need to learn to recognize your "*Binat Halev*" to finally decide what the true answer is that reflects the Torah which you were born with.

SELF-UNDERSTANDING

"*Binat Halev*," our connection with our inner knowledge, is necessary for everything we do in life. When Rav Noach Weinberg taught it in the 48 Ways, he especially focused on one of the most important functions of *Binat Halev* – knowing yourself.

For all of us, it is crucial to be aware of what is going on inside – what is motivating us. Without awareness, we are passengers in a car driven by someone who doesn't know how to drive. An accident is inevitable.

Binat Halev is the tool used to develop our inner ability to understand the different and often conflicting parts that make up who we are.

In the Western world, if someone doesn't understand what is going on inside of him/herself, he/she may seek the help of a psychologist. The psychologist will ask questions about the patient, and guide him/her towards deeper insights. A good psychologist can make a tremendous difference in a person's life.

But if you know how to access and use *Binat Halev*, you can be your own psychologist. Ask the right questions of yourself, and listen with your mind to the answers. Use your *Binat Halev* to judge whether the answers are true answers.

What do you especially need to understand, and what questions will help you obtain that understanding?

The key to self-understanding is for human beings to recognize that they are souls with bodies. The soul wants to be good, to be meaningful, to be great, and to accomplish meaningful things. The body wants rest and relaxation and to avoid pain. The two are in conflict.

What question will help you map out this internal conflict that is in every human being? Ask yourself: what do I "want" and what do I "feel like" doing? "Wants" are long term goals – I want to have a happy family, I want to grow in wisdom. "Feel likes" are short term desires – I feel like watching TV tonight and not talking over family issues, I feel like reading a novel instead of a book that deals with wisdom about life.

We all have many "wants" and many "feel likes." If we write them all down (using Way #3) and see how they conflict with each other, we can understand many of the issues we deal with daily.

A second understanding can come from asking yourself – which of those "wants" is the one that motivates me the most? It isn't enough to know what we "should want" – we all should want to change the world and make it a better place, to achieve real wisdom in life, to have a loving family. What is it you really want most; that your emotions are most connected to? Discovering what is really motivating you is the inner power of a human being.

A third understanding comes from asking yourself – what is preventing you from doing what you really want to do? If you really want to make a difference in the world, and you don't feel that you are doing it, why aren't you? Are you feeling trapped by work? Or do you lack self-confidence? Or are you too lazy to take the time to think about what could be done? Or are you waiting for someone else to inspire you? Or are you rationalizing that nothing can be done anyway?

Any of those could be the correct answer for you, and you won't necessarily know until you ask yourself. Once you know, you can work on changing yourself to do what you want to do.

A DEEPER LEVEL

A person who is on a high spiritual level, and has really mastered the art of *Binat Halev*, will have extra sources of knowledge beyond what other people have. The Rabbis say that a person can't do a good deed without feeling good about it, or a bad deed without feeling bad about it. The person who really knows himself or herself can sometimes use that as a guide for conduct.

An example of this can be found in a story told in the Tanach about King David. David, before he became king, was accused of being a rebel against Shaul the king of the Jewish people at that time. Shaul and his army chased David and his small band of men with the intention of wiping them out. David wasn't a rebel, and Shaul's vendetta was unjustified.

David and his men were hiding in a cave, and Shaul chose that cave to relieve himself. David's men, seeing that Shaul was unguarded and unaware of them, told David that this was his opportunity to save his life by killing his enemy. David went silently behind Shaul and cut off a piece of his garment. The Tanach says: "His heart smote him ... He said to his men 'It would be sacrilegious before *HaShem* for me to do this thing to my Lord, the anointed of *HaShem*.'"

The Malbim's commentary explains what was happening: David was not sure what to do. On the one hand, Shaul was chasing after

David to kill him, and the Torah allows killing in self-defense. On the other hand, Shaul was anointed King by the Almighty – maybe that changes things? David cut off a piece of Shaul's garment, the first step to attacking him, in order to perform a test. Through *Binat Halev* he felt it was wrong, and he knew that it would be wrong to go further in harming Shaul.

If you aren't on such a high level yet, be careful – our desires can affect our ability to be in touch with our inner knowledge. At the least, check your intuitions out with someone else.

These are only some of the most basic points about *Binat Halev*. The subjects for introspection are vast, and each piece you know about yourself makes you a deeper person. You are the most fascinating person that you will ever have a chance to meet, and the only one you can really get to know.

Way · 5

The Power of Awe

¶ Every emotion comes from a perception

¶ The emotion of awe comes from perceiving our smallness in contrast to the majesty and power of G-d and His universe.

¶ We normally feel that emotion when we experience the wonders of nature. We can work on experiencing it on a more regular basis by realizing that everything in the world is a creation of G-d, the awesome Creator and Supervisor of the world.

¶ Learn Torah and do mitzvot with the awe of recognition that they are from the Almighty.

¶ Awe takes you out of the mundaneness of life, the experience of most people, and connects you to the transcendental.

The first four of the 48 Ways dealt with developing the power of the mind: get information, analyze it, put it out into the world, and use your intuition to judge it. Now we turn to emotions and character traits that are crucial for living.

Just like a person can work on developing his or her mind, he or she can work on developing the right emotions. The key to working on those emotions, which we will use throughout the 48 Ways, is to understand the perceptions that cause us to feel something.

We love someone because we perceive the deeper virtues within them, we hate someone because we see their flaws and identify the person with their flaws. We feel angry because we feel that someone has done something wrong to us. If it becomes clear to us that what they did was totally accidental and unintended, the anger will go away. Later in the 48 Ways we will talk more about love and anger, as well as other important emotions.

Way #5, *Aima* in Hebrew ("Awe"), deals with the emotion of awe.

Awe is a feeling that comes from awareness of our smallness and insignificance in the face of overwhelming beauty, distance, and power. Upon seeing the heavens, King David said, "What is man that you should remember him?"

We naturally feel awe when we experience awesome beauty – a snow-capped mountain, a breathtaking sunset. When we see the stars at night, or the vastness of the sea, we feel awe. The thunder and lightning of powerful thunderstorms are awe-inspiring.

In each case, awe comes from feeling the beauty, vastness, and power of the natural world, as compared to our human limitations.

Seemingly this should be an unpleasant experience. To feel alone in a vast crowd of people, or in a city of giant skyscrapers, is not necessarily a pleasurable experience. But to feel alone under the stars, alone staring at the ocean, can be beautiful and pleasurable.

Why? Because when we see the beauty of a snow-capped mountain, the vastness of the sea, or the power of a thunderstorm, we are experiencing a connection with G-d.

We can see this if we ask ourselves: what am I feeling when I appreciate the beauty of the mountains or the vastness of the sea? A large mountain is just lots of dirt and stones piled together. An ocean is just a lot of water. What is pleasurable about more dirt or more water? It is an awareness that the mountain and the sea are creations of G-d, and I appreciate His immense power, a power that can throw up a mountain or stretch out a sea.

In the face of that power, our body steps out of the picture, and we experience the transcendental pleasure of the soul having a G-dly experience.

We aren't necessarily conscious of the fact that the experience of awe we are having is an encounter with G-d. The awesome power of nature works on us even when we aren't thinking about it.

But if you think consciously about what you are experiencing, you can appreciate it so much more!

And not only that, but you can experience awe without having to go away for a vacation. The world that G-d created is truly awesome.

The table in front of you is actually made up of innumerable subatomic particles flying around at the speed of light. We see from the power of the atomic bomb that there is enough power in even a small chunk of the world to blow up a city.

We live in a galaxy that stretches millions of light-years in a universe of trillions of stars. Each star is a ball of energy beyond our imagination.

The human body, with millions of complex parts that work together, is more complex by many magnitudes than anything a human being can create. Even when I pick up my arm, I can feel awe at how my brain chooses among the millions of nerves and muscles to put my decision to raise up my arm into practice.

A shortcut to awe is to realize that the Eternal, the Creator and Supervisor of the World, is always taking care of us. Everything that happens to us represents a decision by G-d about what we need for our growth.

When you learn Torah or do mitzvot, use this awareness. If G-d, who has such great power, gave us a Torah and commanded us to do mitzvot, they must have great depth and significance! When you pray, appreciate the awesomeness of having contact with the Creator of the world.

Working on this awareness – increasing the awe we have – not only increases our pleasure. It is a way to understand the reality of existence, to get out of routine and boredom. Thoreau, the American philosopher, said "the mass of men lead lives of quiet desperation." They get involved in pettiness, and find life boring and unsatisfying. A person who feels the awesomeness of life never has to feel that. He or she knows that everyday life is full of meaning and importance. As Star Wars popularized, "the Force is always with you."

Way · 6

Embracing Fear

¶ The word "to fear" in Hebrew is related to the word "to see." Fear comes from seeing the consequences of our action and inaction, both in this world and the World-to-Come.

¶ In order to see consequences, rather than ignore them, we must make an effort to pay attention to them. G-d will not force us to fear Him by making the consequences impossible to ignore.

¶ To acknowledge and embrace the positive aspect of fear, recognize that fear is good for us. It makes us feel alive. It forces us to use our potential. It prevents us from giving in to the desires of the body.

¶ Fight against "the ostrich syndrome," the desire of human beings to not notice the potential consequences of how we are living. Use the fear of those consequences to motivate us to work on growth.

¶ Fear the consequences that G-d promises if the Jewish people do not return to Him, and use that fear as a motivation to reach out to them.

Way #6 is "Embracing Fear." The Rabbis are telling us that having the emotion of fear is an essential tool for living.

That certainly seems to go against our natural inclination. Franklin D. Roosevelt, the American President, said "We have nothing to fear but fear itself." Fear is a painful emotion that we try to avoid. Even though fear of G-d is one of the mitzvot that we are obligated to have on a constant basis, it is probably the one we are most likely to ignore.

So why is it essential for living?

First, we need to define "fear." The word "fear," *yira* in Hebrew, is related to the Hebrew word "to see." Fear is an emotion that comes from seeing consequences. If you were going across Victoria Falls on a tightrope, you would have fear. If you were ready to sign on a million-dollar business deal, you would fear anything that could break up the deal.

Life itself is full of consequences. Life is a tremendous good. Sickness, accident, war, and crime can cut it short. Bad choices, divorce, economic difficulties, non-fatal sickness and accidents can make life more difficult and painful. If we look at those consequences, we can feel fear for ourselves, our family and those we are close to.

Observant Jews understand that G-d has all the power to control the consequences, for good or for bad. And these consequences aren't limited to this life. There is a World-to-Come, with great reward for those who are keeping Torah, negative consequences for those who are not. Fear of losing out on some of that reward or suffering some of those consequences is very tangible to those who see the World-to-Come as real.

When we "see" potential consequences, for good or bad, we have no choice but to fear. But our Sages tell us that "seeing" those consequences is totally our choice. The Talmud says: "Everything is in the hands of G-d except fear of G-d" – if you don't want to see the consequences of G-d's control of the world, the Almighty promises that He won't force you.

But if it is our choice, why should we choose it? Why would we want to see those consequences and feel fear? Isn't fear painful? Doesn't it limit us from doing what we really want to do? Who would want to live in Russia under Stalin or in China under Mao?

If we want to expand our capacity to fear (and the Sages say it is essential for living), we have to appreciate what is good about it.

It is true that fear is painful, but people will still pay to have it. The mountain climber, race-car driver, and skydiver each invest money and time in doing fearful things. The less courageous of us also experience some vicarious fear by going to horror movies, gambling at casinos, and riding roller coasters.

How does this affect us? It makes us appreciate life more. Every moment counts. Life depends on making the right decisions and avoiding the wrong ones all the time.

Many of these fears are lacking purpose and are inadvisable. Is it worth taking the chance of dying to climb Mount Everest? Will the money you win or lose at the casino change your life in a permanent way? Yet while someone is experiencing these fears, he or she feels very alive, which is a tremendous pleasure.

Fear of G-d is the way to get that pleasure in a way that changes your life for the better.

In the world G-d created, everything is important. In Pirke Avos, it says: "Do not be scornful of any person and do not be disdainful of anything, for there is no person without his hour and there is nothing without its place." Because everything has a purpose, every moment is an opportunity for benefit or loss. The Rabbis say that a person can acquire his World-to-Come in one moment, through one unexpected good act.

If you have fear – the awareness of the consequences of every moment – ordinary life has the excitement of climbing a mountain or racing a car. Nothing is boring or useless to the person who is really in touch with G-d.

But even so, isn't it true that fear of G-d prevents you from doing a lot of things you might feel like doing? If there are negative consequences to wasting time, you can't do it any more – no more sleeping in! If there are negative consequences to being dishonest, you will have to be honest – no more hiding some of the facts about your company in order to make that business deal! And even though you may want to use your time productively and to be honest in business, why put yourself in a situation where you feel forced to?

The answer is that there are many things in life we might feel like doing but don't really want to do. Many of them can seriously affect our lives. A drug addict *feels* like taking drugs, but he doesn't *want* to. He knows it isn't productive. But his body forces him to do it. When he hits bottom, the fear of losing his job and his marriage may be the only thing that will give him the strength to fight his addiction.

Like the drug addict, we are all being pushed by the body to do things that aren't good for us. We want to gain wisdom, to reach our potential, to change the world. But the body stands in the way, promoting distraction, laziness and complacency. Fear of G-d pushes us to fear the consequences of not making the effort to achieve these goals, and gives us the motivation to fight the body and to achieve them.

Bottom line: Fear of G-d is different from other fears because G-d only wants us to do what is good for us. The fact that He sets up positive consequences for doing those things and negative consequences for doing negative things is only to help us get the most out of life.

Like everything else in Judaism, it isn't all or nothing. There are times when, even though there are negative consequences, you will waste time and even be dishonest. But working on developing a fear of G-d, an awareness of those consequences, will help you improve over time. And growth is what life is about.

Once you see the potential value of having fear, how do you work on it? Be aware of the pitfalls of life, and see how easy it is to fall into them. Use fear to motivate yourself to study how to avoid them. Our natural tendency is what Rav Noach Weinberg called "the ostrich syndrome." We put our head in the ground and ignore consequences. Does it matter if I ignore my spouse or my kids? Does it matter if I don't put more effort into learning or praying? Does it matter if I waste my time surfing the Internet? When I consider possible consequences in this world or the World-to-Come, I will make more of an effort to care for the people around me, work on growing in wisdom and personal development. I will focus on what is really important, because I know G-d wants me to do what is really important, even if He has to scare me to get me to accomplish it.

Our Sages said that fear can bring the final redemption. In the Talmud, it says: "Rabbi Eliezer said: if Israel does *teshuva*, they will be redeemed, and if not, they will not be redeemed. Rabbi Yehoshua said to him: if they don't do *teshuva* ... G-d will stand up against them a king whose decrees are as harsh as Haman's, and Israel will do *teshuva* and return to the good."

When people are afraid, they change and turn back to G-d. If necessary, the Almighty will scare us with a ruler as harsh as Haman, who decreed to wipe out the Jews. Be scared of that possibility. Use it as a motivating force to work to get the Jewish people to come back to G-d now.

Way · 7

Living with Humility

¶ Humility is not the same as having a low self-image. Moshe was called by the Torah "the humblest man on the face of the earth," and he was a charismatic leader who fought for what he believed.

¶ Humility is recognizing that you and your personal concerns don't matter. G-d and His cause is what matters.

¶ Examine your motivations: are you doing what you are doing only for yourself or for a greater cause?

¶ Looking at issues objectively helps you to achieve humility.

¶ Humility is the key to leadership, because a leader can focus on what needs to be done, not on self-gain or self-interest.

We all know humility is a virtue. After all, doesn't it say that Moshe our teacher was the humblest man on the face of the earth? When the Rabbis list "Humility" in the 48 Ways as an essential element for living and acquiring Torah, they aren't telling us something we didn't know.

But what is the virtue of humility and how do we work on acquiring it? That is more of a problem. Is humility, as many in the secular world think, the quality of being shy and self-effacing? Is the humble person the person who slithers into the room and slithers out, without making an impression?

It can't be that, because Moshe was a dynamic leader who stood up against Pharaoh and the Jewish people, and even against G-d on occasion. His humility did not rob him of charisma or leadership ability.

So what is humility? Humility is the quality of recognizing that you and your personal concerns don't matter. G-d and His cause is what matters.

This is a very high level to reach. Like any goal in Judaism, no one gets there all at once.

A simple way to start would be to ask yourself: what is my cause? What goal is motivating me? Is it something for myself, or is there a greater meaning to it? Am I working to have a lot of material comforts or to support my family and build a Jewish home? If you are engaged in a profession that helps others, such as a doctor or a teacher, is your goal to get respect from society or to really help others? If you are a creative person, a writer or an artist, is your goal to be recognized by society or to help humanity by teaching or entertaining them?

The more your goal is directed at something outside yourself, the more humility you will have.

But not all goals outside of yourself will have the same capacity to help you grow in humility. The person who is living for his or her family will certainly have a degree of humility. But, even though family is important, it doesn't take all your time and energy. There is still a lot of time to think and worry about yourself.

The more your efforts are directed at an ultimate cause, the more humility you will have. Help your family, but go on to help your community. Help your community, but go on to help the Jewish people as a whole. Help the Jewish people, but do it because it is the Almighty's will and not just what *you* want to do.

Moshe, the man who totally threw himself into the cause of the Almighty, was the most humble man in the world.

It isn't easy to identify your cause and commit yourself to it. The body, that part of yourself which is always worrying about itself, makes it hard. But there are stepping stones, tools you can work on to increase your level of humility. Each one helps distance you from the body and its desires, to a degree, and moves you towards the humility that is necessary to find your cause.

Learn to be objective, to use your mind to examine an issue or deal with a problem. Don't operate on the basis of what you feel.

Objectivity leads to humbleness, because what is true and what is right are important, not what is good for you.

When you hear an idea, examine it objectively: is it true? Don't make your first reaction: do I like this or not?

A way to be more objective is to ask: what should someone else do about this? Should other people set a time in their day to learn more? Should some other couple make a rule never to argue in front of their children?

Work on spending more time in prayer and learning Torah. When you are talking with G-d, or accessing His wisdom, it gets you out of yourself.

Do the right thing because it's right, even if it doesn't pay any immediate benefits. Go to a wedding or a funeral even if no one will notice that you are there. By focusing on what is right, instead of what is in your interest, you develop the consciousness of a humble person.

Humility is not just a good thing. It can do amazing things for you. A humble person can be a leader because the cause is what matters, not the pain involved in doing it. When he sees something that needs to be done, he does it. When he sees that he needs the help of others, he calls them to help out. If a plan is needed, he makes a plan. If an organization is needed, he builds an organization. If his efforts fail, he tries again. And that applies to women as well as men.

Every man and woman has times when they need to lead, in their family or in their community. The Jewish people need to be a light to the nations, to lead the world back to G-d. May we have the humility to embrace our cause and live for it.

Way · 8

Living with Joy

¶ Joy is a positive energizing emotion that comes now from the anticipation of great future pleasures.

¶ Joy is not happiness and happiness is not joy. Happiness comes from appreciating the good that you have, while joy comes from taking pleasure in the even greater good that is to come in the future.

¶ Joy is an emotion that can be worked on and developed. Although we occasionally feel joy that comes naturally from events in our lives promising great future benefits, we can feel it on a constant basis by realizing that the world G-d created is full of opportunities for joy.

¶ Since joy gives us energy and allows us to serve G-d more effectively, it is an obligation. The Torah says that we were sent into exile because we didn't serve G-d with joy.

¶ Since it is an obligation, working on it is hard. But it is a crucial tool for greater connection to G-d and even for prophecy.

The Hebrew term for Way #8 is *Simcha*, or "Joy." We can all understand the benefits of joy. When we feel it, we are ready to take on anything in the world. Life is great, the problems of life seem manageable. We act more effectively, relate to people better, and are able to think in a clearer way.

So shouldn't we have it all the time?

In fact, the Torah does command us to have it all the time. We are supposed to do mitzvot with joy. In the book of Devarim, G-d says that the reason for the long exile that we are in is not that we didn't serve G-d back in Second Temple times, but that we didn't do it with joy.

So why don't we have it all the time? The answer is because it is an emotion. And we think emotions are happenings, we either feel them or we don't. They aren't something we can control and work on. If something happens to me – I have a child, I got a promotion at work – I feel joy. When I am under financial pressure, when I am arguing with my spouse or one of my kids is sick, I'm not feeling joy.

The Jewish understanding is that emotions can be worked on. And the key to working on them is to have a definition of what causes them. To work on "joy," we have to know what "joy" is.

Definition: Joy is a pleasurable, energizing emotion that comes now from the anticipation of great future pleasures.

How can we see that? If you received an email informing you that you won the lottery, and you knew it was real, not a scam, you would feel joy. Why? At that moment, nothing was different in your life. You had no more money than you had a minute ago. But the expectation of having that money in the future, and what you could do with it, propelled you into joy.

When you got married, or had your first child, it was the expectation of the future pleasure that would be coming your way that gave you joy.

Joy and happiness are not the same thing. Happiness is another of the 48 Ways, *Sameach B'helko*, "Happy in His Portion." It is a passive pleasurable feeling that comes from appreciating what you have – good health, a family, a community. It is a foundation feeling that a person needs to have in order to go further. But it won't, on its own, push you to do something.

In contrast, joy is future-oriented, and actively pushes you to make that future a reality.

In the same way, "sadness," the opposite of happiness, is a passive feeling that things aren't good. "Depression," the opposite of joy, is much worse. The feeling that everything is bad and getting worse drives a person into the ground.

When something happens, like winning a lottery or having a child, we are so aware of the future good that we don't need to focus on it, we feel joy naturally. But we can train ourselves to see the potential good in our daily lives, because simply being alive is a cause for joy.

When you wake up, say *Modeh Ani*. Thank G-d for the fact that you are alive, and there will be a lot of pleasure coming your way in the new day. There is good food, fresh air, contact with people you love, and the opportunity to accomplish some of your goals. Even if some of those are lacking in any particular day, and even if you have problems and worries, the benefits of living far outweigh the negatives.

But there are even deeper pleasures that are available all the time. You can take pleasure in the fact that you are Jewish, part of the chosen people, G-d's army. You can take pleasure in the fact that you have a Jewish family and Jewish children, and that you are contributing to the mission of the Jewish people, rather than assimilating. You can take pleasure in the fact that you have some connection to His Torah, His instructions on how to live. You can take pleasure in the mitzvot that you do – educating your children, giving charity, prayer, learning Torah. All these things are not only good things now, but continue to make your life better and promise great rewards in the World-to-Come.

Negative feelings or events shouldn't keep you from having joy. If you received the letter about the lottery, you would feel joy even if you were sick in bed or the wrong person had been elected President. The goodness of life is always there, even in bad times.

Since joy is a powerful pleasure, it has powerful counterfeits. You might think you are feeling joy at the New Year's Eve party, or when your team won the World Series. The key to knowing whether this is real joy is to ask yourself – what is the good I am expecting? It isn't hard to see that your life will not change because of the New Year's Eve party or because of the World Series. False joy ends up draining you, when you realize that nothing has changed. New Year's Eve is a leading night for suicides.

Even real joy – you won the lottery, you graduated from university – won't get you anywhere if you don't use it to take positive steps toward the future. If, a year later, you have wasted all your money or you have not used your degree in a positive way, you are likely to get as depressed as you were joyous before.

It is important to keep reminding yourself of these principles.

47

Like any positive emotion, joy takes work. Our default position is to give in to the laziness of the body, which would rather be bored, or even depressed. For the body, joy can be too much effort.

The Rabbis say, "Prophecy only comes to a person who has joy." When you have joy, you are in touch with G-d, because you know that the world is His gift to you. You understand that it is all for your pleasure. That is why the students who studied to become prophets at the time of the First Temple sat with musical instruments in front of them. They would play, it would lift their souls up to joy, and they could hear what G-d wanted to communicate to them.

We don't have prophecy today, but G-d is always communicating with us. He talks to us through His Torah, through events in our lives, and through thoughts that come to us. When you feel joy, it will be easier to ask yourself – what does the Almighty want to tell me?

Way · 9

Purity of Mind and Emotion

❡ Purity, as a tool for living, means to have all your capabilities – mind, emotions and will – completely focused and operating to their full extent.

❡ A prerequisite to doing this is to realize that, just as you have control of your hand, you have the potential to control your mind, your emotions, and your will.

❡ "Intellectual purity" means to control your mind, one thought at a time – don't be "scattered." It also means that when you think something, take it seriously – don't be a "dilettante."

❡ "Emotional purity" means to control your emotions, one emotion at a time. Choose the emotion that is most productive at that time. It also means to work on feeling an emotion deeply.

❡ "Goal purity" means to control your will, and focus on one goal at a time. It also means to put all your efforts into that goal in order to accomplish it.

My teacher, Rabbi Noach Weinberg, used to say that the 48 Ways are so powerful that when the non-Jewish world discovers even one of them, they make a whole religion or philosophy out of it. His example was Way #9, which in Hebrew is *Tahara*, meaning "Purity." He pointed out that one aspect of the Way, "intellectual purity," was the basis of transcendental meditation.

But that is only one part of the Way. Another aspect, "emotional purity," is the basis of a psychological movement called "Neuro-linguistic programming." One part of emotional purity is used by Tony Robbins for his famous "Firewalk." And another aspect of purity, "Goal Purity," is used by many business books.

The Hebrew term *tahara*, "purity," means something unadulterated. Pure gold means gold without any impurities. As a tool for living, *tahara* means to use the different aspects of a human being, mind, emotions and will, in a fully concentrated way, with nothing else getting in the way.

To do this, realize that you have the ability to control and direct yourself in any way you desire. If we aren't paralyzed, we have the ability to control our hand, even though we have no idea how we do it. A thought – "I want to move my hand" – somehow creates an electrical impulse from the brain sent down through the nerves to the muscles and – presto! My hand moves!

In the same way, we can control our thoughts – we just have less practice doing it. That's the basis of transcendental meditation. And we can control our emotions, even though we are used to them being out of our control – that's the basis of neuro-linguistic programming and Tony Robbins' Firewalk.

INTELLECTUAL PURITY

The first aspect of purity is intellectual purity, getting control of your mind.

Most of us have a lot of difficulty doing this. Right now, many things are going on in your mind – you are reading this, but you may be noticing the kids in the background, you're worrying whether or not you will get a raise and considering what you should do about it, you are thinking that it is almost lunch-time.

We call a person who has a lot of thoughts passing through his or her mind "scattered." And that can be a problem! You may be distracted and unable to think out an issue to make a decision. Or have trouble listening to what someone is saying even if you want to. You take longer reading that report, or coming up with the correct strategy, or end up getting in an argument with your spouse because your mind drifted to something else and you missed something he or she said. We know how often we begin to think of other things when we are praying to G-d.

We miss a lot of what is going on the world because we don't focus our minds on it. Many psychology experiments have been done to show that people usually see what they think is in front of them, not what is really there, because they don't concentrate. Even concentrating on a plant or a flower, you will see much more than what you realized before. Imagine if you really concentrated on your children!

Transcendental meditation is a technique for focusing your mind. But you can do that without paying all your money to a guru. Just realize – you are the master of your mind like you are the master of your hand! Just like you can control your hand to pick up something on the table, even though you don't know how you do it, you can control your mind to concentrate on the book or person in front of you.

How do we see this is true? When the report is due for tomorrow, we find the ability to concentrate. When we are being told news that we are interested in or feel we really need to know, we concentrate. Why? Because we want to. Our mind responds to what we want, just like our hand does.

So the key to concentrating is deciding you want to make the effort to control your mind. It isn't easy at first. It takes a baby time to learn to walk. When you first started to ride a bicycle, or to drive a shift car, it wasn't easy. But when you kept doing it, you got better at it. In the same way, by working at it, you can train your mind.

Some of the tools of other 48 Ways can help you concentrate. Speaking out loud, or writing things down, from Way #3 ("Using the Power of Speech"), can focus your mind. Way #6, "Embracing Fear" – understanding the consequences of not focusing in this situation – can do it also. Searching for what interests you in the subject you are learning – a later one of the 48 Ways – can help you concentrate, especially when you are learning Torah.

What is the best use you can make of the powers of concentration? The Rabbis quote a line from Tehillim "I keep G-d in front of me always." Take two minutes to concentrate on the fact that G-d is always with us. Do it every day, and concentrating will become easier.

The deepest use of the power of concentration is for meditation.

Not by focusing on a meaningless mantra like TM does. Concentrate your mind on a subject with meaning, like love of G-d.

Another aspect of intellectual purity is to take what your mind says seriously. We are all familiar with the person who says one thing and does another, who says he is on your side but then talks behind your back. But it is even more common for a person to think one thing about life, and then act as if he thinks something completely different. People who do that are "intellectually shallow," or "dilettantes" – they don't take seriously the consequences of what they believe.

We see this all around us. In current events, it might be the person who truly believes that carbon emissions cause global warming and are a menace to the future of the world, and has no problem with jetting off to a vacation in his private plane, using more carbon than the average person uses in a month. In daily life, it might be the person who truly believes that his family is his priority, and spends all his time at the office or away on business trips.

In South Africa, where I live, it is common to meet Jews who believe that there is a G-d, and even believe that Torah is true. But they act in their lives as if He doesn't. In their relationship with their families, or in doing business, they act the same as a person who doesn't believe. A dishonest businessman who is an observant Jew (except when it comes to observing Jewish laws on business practices) is engaging in that type of schizophrenia. He wouldn't act dishonestly if a government inspector was carefully going over his books. Yet he believes in a G-d who is aware of his every action and yet ignores His existence.

In Pirke Avos, it says: "Look deeply at three things and you won't come into the hands of sin: Know what is above you: an eye that sees, an ear that hears, and all your actions are written in a Book." The Sages, who are talking here to observant Jews, say: pay attention to what you believe is true, and see that it is the reality of existence. Only then will your actions match up with your mind.

EMOTIONAL PURITY

Emotions are a key part of a human being. Rav Noach Weinberg's brother, Rabbi Yakov Weinberg of blessed memory, the *Rosh*

HaYeshiva of Ner Yisroel in Baltimore, said: "You cannot trust emotions. You must always judge emotions. But you cannot fulfil yourself as a human being without emotions. Reason cannot motivate; it is sterile. Emotions motivate. But reason must act as a measuring rod to judge your emotions, whether they are appropriate or not. This is what Torah and divine service are all about."

But emotions often seem to us to be out of our control. We feel what we feel, what can we do about it?

The first step in directing emotions, as we have mentioned before, is to know what perceptions cause us to feel different emotions. Anger comes from thinking something wrong is being done, so we can work on anger by realizing the wrong was unintentional or excusable. Joy comes from anticipating great things in the future, so we can raise our level of joy by focusing on what we can expect.

But when we are feeling emotions, we can have difficulty knowing what to do with them. A person can be intellectually scattered, having many thoughts at once, as we said earlier. But we can be "emotionally scattered" as well, having many different emotions at the same time.

For example: When you wake up in the morning, you feel tired. You feel worried about the way things are going at your job. You miss your best friend, who moved to Israel. But you are excited at the fact that you have tickets to the basketball game later. And you are curious about what your teacher will say at the Torah class tonight. You are worried about your persistent health problems, but interested to get up and check what might have happened in the world last night. And these are all happening at the same time!

The emotion you feel most strongly will often dictate how the day goes. If the positive emotions predominate, you say a warm good morning to your spouse and kids and you go into the day with renewed energy. If worry or other negative emotions predominate, you act tense and impatient with your spouse and kids and drag yourself through the day.

It is obvious that happiness and positivity are a better response. But if emotions are "happenings" out of your control, you can't do anything about it – what you feel is what you feel.

This second part of Way #9 – "Purity of Mind and Emotion" – teaches that you don't have to leave it to chance. Just like you can choose your thoughts, you can choose your emotions. This is the basis of secular techniques like neuro-linguistic programming and the power of positive thinking.

How do you do that? You need to realize that, just like you have the ability to control your hand and your mind, you can control your emotions.

When do we see that? A doctor who is involved in serious surgery focuses his emotions on doing a successful job and helping his patient. What if he thought: I am hurting this person, I'm causing him to bleed! Or he was worried about making a mistake and getting a malpractice suit. Or he was distracted by the argument he had with his wife that morning?

In the same way, a mother whose child is having a temper tantrum can say to herself: I am keeping calm. Someone who is late to an important meeting because of an unforeseen traffic jam can still say: let me just concentrate on driving safely.

When the stakes are high enough, we pull the switch to use the emotion that is most productive.

Practice choosing the most productive emotions in your daily life: joy, when you wake up and say *Modeh Ani*; love, for your spouse (we will teach how to work on "love" later in the 48 Ways); patience, with your children; and excitement, when you are learning something new.

It isn't easy to do, but if you work on it, you can grow in control. You don't know how your hand responds to you, but it does. You don't know how your mind responds to you, but you can train it. Your emotions can be trained also, it's just harder.

Once you have control of your emotions, you can work on deepening them. That's what they do in "Firewalk." Shout enough times "I can do it," and you actually can.

Tell yourself "this is really interesting" when you are learning or "I can concentrate" when you are praying.

The Sages interpreted the verse in the Torah, "When a man dies in a tent" (Bamidbar 19:14) as hinting to the study of Torah (yeshivot are called "tents of Torah"). When you are learning Torah, strengthen both your mental concentration and your emotional desire to learn and understand. Shut out the world as if you were dead to it.

The Rambam teaches about love of G-d: "What is the love of G-d that is fitting? It is to love the Almighty with a great, exceeding, mighty, very fierce love so that his soul is tied to the love of G-d and he finds himself thinking about it always like a person who is sick with love." Choosing carefully his words, he is giving stepping stones to deepening emotions – from "great" to "exceeding" to "mighty" to "very" to "very fierce" to being "sick with love." That is what we are supposed to be working on.

Listen to Jewish motivational speakers, listen to Jewish music based on Tehillim. If you know what the words mean, and connect them to the music, you can deepen your love of G-d.

GOAL PURITY

Many years ago, I read a book by a motivational writer named Napoleon Hill called "Think and Grow Rich." One of his most basic principles was: if you want to become rich, you have to be totally focused on it. Eat, drink and sleep with the idea of becoming rich.

Hill was a man with wisdom, even though his goal was a mistaken one. His single-minded focus on getting rich led him to appreciate a lot of the other 48 Ways, which all can be used for secular purposes. To get a goal accomplished, you need to be single-mindedly committed to it. Being "scattered" in goals can be as damaging as being "scattered" in mind or emotions.

Although we have different goals at different times in life, when we are engaged in an activity leading to one of those goals, we need to be single-minded about it. When learning Torah, focus on your goal – remembering, understanding – and not on preparing in your mind for the business meeting you are having in a few hours. When you are at that business meeting, focus on your goal – to successfully make the deal, or work out a new strategy – and not on rethinking the important idea in life you learned a few hours ago. When you get home, focus on your wife and children and what they need, and not on tomorrow's schedule.

The real power of a human being comes when all your sub-goals are focused on one mega-goal. Think out what you are living for, and put all your efforts – learning, working, family – into that. In Pirke Avos it says "all your actions (eating, drinking, sleeping) should be for the sake of G-d (in order to connect with G-d and His purpose)."

In "Path of the Just," Rabbi Moshe Chaim Luzzatto says: "The foundation of all wisdoms and the root of pure service of G-d is for a person to know what his obligation in the world is and to what he should put his vision and ambition in everything he does all the days of his life." He says that a person needs to have one goal, and that goal should be understood intellectually ("vision") and cared about emotionally ("ambition"). And he tells us that the Sages have expressed what that one goal is: "human beings were only created to take pleasure in G-d."

May we have G-d's help to use all our powers to make use of the multi-faceted world He has created for us to take pleasure in Him.

Way · 10

Seeking Wisdom from the Wise

❡ We wouldn't build a bridge based only on our own wisdom. To build a life, which is more complicated than a bridge, we need to access the wisdom of others.

❡ Seek wisdom from every human being. "Who is the wise man? The one who learns from every person."

❡ Have at your fingertips the questions you have about life, and ask them to any wise person you meet.

❡ If possible, have one wise person who is your special teacher, so that you don't "shop around" for the answers that you would like to hear.

❡ If that is not possible, have one person that you specially go to for advice, even if he isn't necessarily wiser than you. As an objective outsider, he can see things that you, with your subjectivity about yourself, might not be able to see.

Ways 10–12 deal with key relationships in your life. One of the most important ways to get wisdom is to be able to access the wisdom of others. That is the subject of Way #10 – "Seeking Wisdom from the Wise." Seek out wise people and learn to benefit from their wisdom.

This isn't as easy as it sounds. We have a natural resistance to learning from others. Women notice that in men – as the joke goes,

"Why were the Jews lost in the desert for 40 years? Because the men didn't want to ask directions."

Why that resistance? We want to think we know everything. What we don't know, we think "I'll learn myself." Pride effects every human being, and learning from someone else is a humbling experience.

To overcome that resistance, we need to appreciate the need to learn from people. To build a bridge, you would need to learn engineering from others. Is life less complicated than a bridge? We think we can learn about life from experience, but would you make investment decisions that way?

Rav Noach Weinberg used to quote the proverb: "A fool learns from his own mistakes, a wise man learns from the mistakes of others." Learning from your own mistakes can include divorces, choosing the wrong career, spending the best years of your life chasing money instead of meaning. These can be very painful experiences, and often we get the wrong lessons. We say: forget about marriage, it doesn't work, instead of: I chose based on the wrong standards, or I didn't study how to make marriage work.

So you need to learn from others. Who do you learn from? In Pirke Avos, it says: "Who is the wise man? The one who learns from everyone."

Look at people five, ten, or twenty years older, and try to figure out: what do they know that I need to know? When you are a guest at someone's home, or hosting someone, don't spend the time telling people about your life – ask them about their lives. If they have had unique experiences, ask them what they learned from those experiences.

Appreciate older people, who have had many experiences in life. Even if they don't know as much as you about computers or cellphones, they have dealt with many things that are more important. The Rabbis say: Stand even for an elderly non-Jew, because "how many acts of G-d has he seen!"

The best people to learn from are wise people, especially people who have learned from the Torah, G-d's book of wisdom. When you meet a wise man, have at your fingertips the questions you want clarity on.

Rav Noach suggested as an exercise: write down five questions you would ask if you met the wisest man in the world. What's the ultimate meaning of life, how do I juggle work and Torah study, what's the key factor in choosing a school for my children? Whatever your questions are, when you meet a wise man, even if he isn't the wisest in the world, ask him.

We can gain wisdom from any person, and especially from wise people, but the Rabbis say: "Make for yourself a teacher." Designate someone as a special teacher that you go to with all your life questions.

Why have one special teacher? In South Africa, where I live, people love to go from rabbi to rabbi! What's wrong with that? The answer is that, if you go to many people, you pick and choose. You select the person who will tell you what you want to hear, or go to many people until one of them tells you what you want to hear.

Choosing one teacher doesn't mean you have to follow blindly whatever he says. But once you have selected someone as your special teacher, you have to take his words seriously. If you disagree with him, you have to think out seriously why you disagree and argue it out with him. You can't just say, like we normally do – that is his opinion, and I think differently.

When you choose your teacher, look for a Torah scholar, who understands what life is about from the ultimate source. But you also have to feel that he is selfless, interested in you, with no hidden agendas. He must have sensitivity and judgment with people. Most important, he has to be available to you. If the greatest Torah scholar in town is so busy that he doesn't have time to talk with you and understand your problems, find the second greatest.

It is not always easy or possible for us to find such a special teacher. But the Rabbis went so far as to say, about the person who can't find a teacher: "Make for yourself a teacher, even if he is smaller in wisdom than you." But what good is a teacher who knows less than you?

The Sages understood that even the wisest people have poor judgment about issues that affect them emotionally. They gave as an example the story of King Solomon and Shimi ben Gera. Shimi was head of the Sanhedrin during the reign of King David. He joined with King David's son Avshalom in a revolt against David. When King David was running away from Avshalom, Shimi came out and publicly cursed the King.

Cursing a King is a death penalty offense. But when David defeated Avshalom and returned, he didn't want to be seen as coming back to take revenge. He swore to Shimi that he wouldn't kill him. He even made Shimi, who was a wise man, the teacher of Solomon, the son who would be the future king.

David felt that Shimi should be punished for cursing the King. On his deathbed, he commanded Solomon to find a pretext to execute Shimi. Solomon, who asked for and was given by G-d wisdom greater than any other man, was able to find a pretext and had Shimi executed.

Soon after that, Solomon made his first big mistake by marrying the daughter of Pharaoh of Egypt. He certainly had strong reasons why he thought it was the right thing, but she was a headstrong lady who started the spiritual decline of the Jewish people.

The Rabbis made a connection between the two events. They said: "Always a person should live in the place of his teacher, because if Solomon had not killed Shimi, he would never have married Pharaoh's daughter." Solomon was the wisest man in the world. Seemingly he wouldn't need the advice of a lesser wise man. But Shimi could be objective. Had he been alive, he would have convinced Solomon that it was a bad idea.

So if you can't find the ideal teacher, find someone you respect and make him or her your teacher. He or she can be objective where you can't be.

Way · 11

Having a Real Friend

❧ Having a friend is a crucial relationship for wisdom. A friend can understand you and advise you in a way a teacher might not be able to do.

❧ Friendship needs to be a permanent relationship. You can only trust someone who is committed to you. You can't trust a "friend" on Facebook to understand you or be committed to your growth.

❧ Since friendship requires mutual commitment and responsibility, you can't have many friends.

❧ The Sages say "buy yourself a friend." Choose who you can gain the most from and make that person your friend with gifts of wisdom and concern.

❧ To change the world, you need to have good friends. A team working together is exponentially more powerful than an individual working alone.

To grow in wisdom, you need relationships with other people. Way #10 – "Seeking Wisdom from the Wise," dealt with your relationship to a teacher, someone above you in wisdom. The Hebrew title for Way #11 is *Dikduk Chaverim*, literally "careful analysis with friends," and speaks about your relationship with a friend, someone who is on the same level as you.

We have friends for many reasons. We don't want to be lonely, we want to be part of the "in-crowd," we want to have people to do things with. But the relationship with friends that this 48 Way is talking about is for the same purpose as your relationship with a teacher. A real friend is a source of wisdom. You grow in wisdom by sharing wisdom with each other in a discussion-style atmosphere.

The fact that your Facebook acquaintances are called "friends" tells us something about the secular view of friendship. Friendship, in the secular world, is whoever you have a pleasant relationship with. It includes not only people you have never met on Facebook, but your school acquaintances, your drinking buddies, your poker partners, the moms of your son's playgroup, the people in your shul community.

There is nothing wrong with any of these relationships, but they are not what the Rabbis meant by a "friend."

We have a mitzvah to love every Jew. That doesn't mean to be friends with every Jew. You can have lots of pleasurable acquaintances, but only a few friends.

What is a real friend?

Real friendship is a permanent relationship. Just like the relationship with a spouse is permanent, except in disastrous situations, and a relationship with a child is permanent, your relationship with a friend should be permanent.

A friend should be someone on an equal level to you, who can give you wisdom on the issues you are bothered by, and can receive wisdom from you. Because you are committed to each other, you can have deep conversations, share innermost values and aspirations, and discuss your personal problems. If you can't tell him or her your innermost anxieties, he or she isn't a friend.

A true friend will argue with you when he thinks you are doing the wrong thing, support you when you are doing the right thing, and go over with you the things you are unclear about so that you can understand them better.

You can't be this sort of friend with your teacher, because you take wisdom from him but don't directly give him wisdom (indirectly, teachers learn a lot from their students, as we will talk about in the next 48 Way). You can't be this sort of friend with your student, someone who is needing your help all the time, but can't give back.

In Judaism, the ideal for learning is to have a study partner, "chavruta," to discuss wisdom together. Even more ideal is if this study partner is your friend. In the Talmud, it calls a Torah scholar who is on the same level as another Torah scholar a *talmid chaver*, a "student friend."

Because a real friend is a serious relationship, you can't have too many people that you have that relationship with. The Rabbis say in Pirke Avos, "buy a friend." What they mean is that, although you should be pleasant to and care about many people, you should choose who you want to make a friend. Choose the person with the most wisdom, the best values, an ability to care, a sense of idealism.

This is not being mercenary. We have a responsibility to help people, irrespective of whether they can benefit us or not. But we make our permanent relationships on the basis of what the other person can do for us. You choose your wife or husband based on what you can get out of it, rather than choosing the spouse who is most in need of your help. So it should be with friends.

Once you have chosen, as in marriage, you have to accept the responsibility that comes with it, the love, loyalty, and concern for the other's welfare.

How do you "buy" a friend? Obviously not with money! You "buy" friends through caring about their situation and helping them. By giving your care and wisdom to them, you create the relationship that will help you in your own growth.

Having this relationship is important for the person who wants to be great and change the world. Every human being has talents and faults. Because of the talents we don't have, and the faults we do have, changing the world can't be done by an individual. It can only be done by a team. If the members of the team are not friends, the team can easily break apart. A team of real friends, committed to each other, can accomplish great things that no person could accomplish alone.

Way · 12

Growth through Teaching: The Questioning of Students

❡ Teaching others is a cause and a responsibility. If you know the cure for cancer, you are a murderer if you don't teach it. If you know how to help people be happy or have a good marriage, you are hurting them by withholding your knowledge.

❡ In addition, teaching is a crucial way to gain wisdom. The questions of students force you to clarify your own knowledge and realize what you understand and what you don't understand about whatever you are teaching.

❡ Teach at every opportunity. Don't wait to be perfect at teaching or to have the perfect student.

❡ Teaching means to communicate understanding, not to entertain or preach.

❡ Every Jew who knows Torah has an obligation to teach to those many Jews who don't have Torah. If even one person listens to you, you have changed his or her life forever.

W ay #10 was about the relationship between a person and his teacher. Way #11 was about the relationship between friends. Way #12, referred to in Hebrew as *Pilpul Talmidim*, "The Questioning of Students," deals with a person's relationship with his students. In order to know more about life, you have to teach about life to others.

In Western society, teaching is a profession. In Jewish society, teaching is a responsibility and a cause. It is a commandment to teach your children. The Rambam adds that "It is a mitzvah on every wise man in Israel to teach all students, even if they aren't his children."

It is a common occurrence in religious communities that dentists, lawyers, and businessmen teach classes after working hours on a voluntary basis to fulfil this mitzvah.

It isn't rocket science to understand why teaching is a responsibility. If you knew someone who was giving out a million dollars, no strings attached, to anyone who asked, and you kept that information away from people who really could use the money – how wrong would that be!

If a person knew the cure for cancer, and he didn't want to take the time and effort to teach it over – wouldn't he be considered a murderer?

If you could teach someone how to have a relationship with G-d, how to have a happy marriage, how to be happy and avoid depression, and you didn't have the time to share it, what excuse could you make for that?

If you care about people, you need to teach them. That is why parents are always making an effort to teach their children, because they care.

Teaching is not only a responsibility, it is one of the necessary means to acquire Torah. When you teach something, it forces you to understand the subject better. You find out what parts of it you are unclear about. When students ask their questions they force you to work on those things that you couldn't explain clearly because you were missing some understanding yourself.

The Rabbis say: "I learned a lot from my teachers, and from my friends, but even more from my students."

So how do you go about teaching?

First, accept the need to do it and teach at every opportunity. It doesn't have to be in a class. Just tell over to your friends an idea you heard that you think is important.

Don't wait until you are 100% perfect. You'll never get there. If people ask you questions you don't know the answer to, tell them you'll check it out with a rabbi and get back to them.

Don't wait for the perfect students who are 100% ready to listen.

You will almost never find them. Good teachers tell stories, tell jokes, and ask questions to involve their audience.

Identify what you think people need most to know about. Get together with a group of acquaintances to teach them the 48 Ways. All the Ways deal with ideas for living that people badly need and often don't know about.

Teaching means to communicate what you know and get it into someone else's understanding. It doesn't mean to preach to them or just to entertain. Observant Jews sometimes feel they have an obligation to tell you a *dvar Torah*, a lesson from the Torah, even though they aren't really interested and you aren't really interested. That isn't teaching. Tell others something from the Torah that matters to you and that you think will matter to them.

The ultimate goal of teaching is to teach in such a real fashion that students must ask their questions. That is why the Way is called *Pilpul Talmidim*, "The Questioning of Students." You and your students become partners in learning.

Today, every Jew who knows some Torah, man or woman, has the opportunity to teach crucial ideas for living to those who know less than them. Everyone has family, friends, or acquaintances who can gain from the wisdom of the Torah. Think out how you can reach out to them at a Shabbat table or through a home group.

Don't be put off by the fact that not everyone will be interested. The Rabbis say in Pirke Avos, "Stand up many students." You never know which person will take your words seriously enough to use them to the fullest extent. When you reach out to others, even if many won't listen, if one person listens you've changed his or her life forever for the good.

Way · 13

Searching your Mind for Wisdom with Deliberateness

¶ To be able to use the power of the mind, you have to get the information you learn to stay in your mind, and you have to be able to retrieve it when you need to apply it in living.

¶ Whatever you learn, take time to absorb and remember it. Without doing that, most of what you learn gets lost.

¶ In order to retrieve the stored information when you need it, you must take the time to think and reflect, which requires practice.

¶ The most important question to think about is: what am I living for? Make a regular time in your day or week to think about that question.

¶ The secret to inspiration is to make the effort to think. G-d sends answers to the person who wants to know.

The last three of the 48 Ways have been teaching about wisdom gained through relationships: with your teacher, your friend, or your students. But there is another crucial relationship that is a source of wisdom – your relationship with your own mind.

Way #13 is referred to in Hebrew as *B'Yishuv*. Literally, that means "With Sitting." Its subject is to be slow and deliberate in getting the wisdom we learn lodged securely in our minds, and in probing the wisdom we already have in our minds.

Our mind is an incredible tool, the greatest computer in the world. As we have mentioned before, our mind is programmed with all Torah, everything we need to know about living. But when we are born, the Talmud tells us, we forget it all and have to work on recapturing that knowledge. Through our education and experiences, we get in touch with that wisdom. Once we are in touch with it, we can use it in living.

But getting the information to be processed by the computer, so it can be used in living, is not so easy. The mind blocks retaining most information when we have heard it only one time (We can understand this as a way that G-d helps us – imagine if we remembered every detail of every TV show we have ever seen). To store information in our memory requires an effort.

And even when it is in our memory, we have to be able to access it again when we need it. And since the information we acquired came over many years and through many different sources, it isn't necessarily available to us without effort.

The first step to using the powers of your mind is the Way of *B'Yishuv*. Being willing to take the time to think about what you learn is a necessary prerequisite to committing wisdom to memory, expanding your understanding of it, and applying it.

This isn't as easy as it sounds. To train yourself in thinking is one of the most difficult things for human beings. Henry Ford, the famous inventor, said: "Thinking is the hardest work there is, that is why so few people engage in it." Many of us are untrained in using our minds. But like learning how to ride a bicycle or drive a shift car, with practice we can learn how to do it.

So first you have to be willing to make some time. Set some time in your day to think about something that you have learned.

THE FOUR STEPS OF *B'YISHUV*

The Rabbis say that, whatever you study, learn it four times. They say that G-d created the process of farming to teach us about gaining wisdom, because wisdom is to the soul like food is to the body.

So for learning – the first time is plowing the ground, just getting used to the subject. The second time is planting – get the information into your memory. The third time is harvesting. Ask – what did I learn from this? The fourth time is eating. Ask – what do I do about this?

Don't think you are growing just because you are going through a lot of information. When you plow, without planting and harvesting, the information gets lost. If it is worth the investment of your time to learn it, it is worth remembering it and asking what you learned from it.

When you hear wisdom that seems important to you, take time to remember it. In the Talmud, we see incidents where a Sage, hearing a new wisdom idea, repeated it to himself on the spot 40 times!

Just as important, take the time to think about it. Do you agree? Does it change your world-view? What should you do about it? Going through this process plants the idea in your mind in a much deeper way than if you listened to it without examining it.

APPLYING *B'YISHUV*

Once information is stored in your mind, learn to use your mind as a research tool for everything you do. We have all learned from Google that there are large amounts of information available if you know what to search for. You can learn to search your own mind to access the information you need in order to accept, reject, analyze, and deepen your understanding of any idea that is important in your life.

Becoming an expert in asking the right questions is dealt with in Way #44 – "The Key to Unlocking Your Mind: Asking and Answering" and Way #45 – "The Key to Creativity: Hearing and Adding On." But the start to accessing the powers of your mind is Way #13. By taking the time to think out something, you can open the gate to using the wisdom you have already achieved.

The situations in life to use this way of *B'Yishuv* are almost endless. Here are a few:

The Rabbis say in Pirke Avos: Be deliberate in making decisions. That includes the decisions we make every day of our lives. Think: what am I going to do in the coming day, and why? Are they good things to do? Is there something else that would be better?

When you are being criticized, take time think about it, instead of just reacting. When you are having an argument, at your work or with your spouse, think out what the other person is saying instead of hurrying to give an answer. Why might he/she be right? How do I know that he/she is wrong?

"Learn your life." Go over your day each night. What did you do, what did you learn about life from what you did that day?

Every human being has moments of clarity. When you understand something – for instance, during Yom Kippur – don't just go on. You will forget it unless you take some time to think about it.

The most important thing to be deliberate in is: What am I living for?

Thinking about what you are living for isn't easy. In "Path of the Just," Rav Moshe Chaim Luzzatto says that this is the #1 goal of the "*yetzer hara*," "the evil inclination" – to keep you from thinking. He says that the *yetzer hara* realizes that, if people will spend only a few minutes thinking about their goals in life and comparing it to how they are living, they would start to change. Better keep them busy with work and entertainment.

So set a few minutes every day to ask yourself what your goals are in life. And if you can't do it every day, then once a week. Or at least once a month.

THE MOST PROFOUND APPLICATION OF B'YISHUV

The most profound application of *B'Yishuv* comes from realizing that the source of all wisdom is the Almighty. When you are thinking out something you learned, or a problem that you have, you are first connecting with all the information you have connected to in your life, from education or experience. But there is much more information in the computer – everything you were taught in your mother's womb about living. If you make the effort to understand, the Almighty can connect you with that information, and you can come up with new insights that you never learned about from others.

That is why Thomas Edison, the famous inventor, said that genius is 99% perspiration and 1% inspiration. The Jewish people also understood that principle. Rabbi Elazar ben Arach, the most creative student of Rabban Yochanan ben Zakkai, was described by his teacher in Pirke Avos as "an ever-flowing spring of water." Just like spring water comes from a source deep in the ground, inspiration flows from the Almighty to the one He wants to give it to. More than any of his colleagues, Rabbi Elazar was receiving G-d's inspiration constantly and coming up with new and deeper understandings of Torah. Yet Rabbi Elazar was also quoted in Pirke Avos as teaching "Be intensely diligent in the study of Torah." He knew that inspiration was the reward given for the effort a person makes to learn and understand.

The Rabbis also said, about understanding Torah: "If someone says I tried, but I didn't find the answer, don't believe him." If you make the effort to use your mind to understand, the Almighty will send you the answer.

Way · 14

Accessing the Written Law

❡ The Written Law (Mikra) and the Oral Law (Mishne) are the two parts of G-d's communication to us about how to live.

❡ If G-d wants to communicate with us, it is crazy not to make the effort to know what He wants to communicate. Even though the Written Law is difficult, and the Oral Law even more so, we need to make a plan to learn as much of it as we can.

❡ The Written Law gives us the big picture, the purpose of man and how human beings can relate to G-d. The Oral Law gives us all the details of actually putting these ideas into practice.

❡ To get wisdom from the Torah, we have to treat it as from G-d. Everything in the Torah is true, moral, and relevant. Don't take the written Torah as stories or as ideas applicable only to ancient times. Don't take the Oral Law as the work of ancient Rabbis out-of-touch with the modern world.

❡ Use the Written and Oral Laws as research tools. When you know them well enough, you can use them to look into any issues you are facing in your life.

Wisdom about life comes to us in many ways, but what could be a more direct way of accessing wisdom than the Torah that the Almighty gave us? That is why the 48 Ways includes #14 – "Accessing the Written Law," and #15 – "Accessing the Oral Law." We can seek wisdom from a teacher, a friend, a student, or from our own inner knowledge (Ways #10–13). But nothing is as 100% accurate as learning it from the Creator Himself.

Our Torah is a set of books and laws with deep spiritual power to influence us. In "The Way of G-d," Rabbi Moshe Chaim Luzzatto speaks of the Torah as the primary way for G-d to channel His spiritual energy to us. This is the spiritual energy that anyone feels who learns in a yeshiva.

But the aspect of Torah that the 48 Ways is referring to here is the Torah as the ultimate wisdom book. All of the Torah is called "*Torat Chaim*," "Instructions for Living." Each part of it is teaching, in different ways, the wisdom we need to know to lead our lives successfully.

Since G-d gave us instructions for living, it goes without saying we should make the effort to know it. If you really wanted to be an accountant, and one thick and difficult to understand textbook would tell you what you needed to know, you wouldn't let yourself be held back by the fact that it is difficult. You would read it as many times as necessary to know it.

Life is more complex and more important than accounting. We need to make a plan for ourselves: how am I going to know the Almighty's Torah?

Realize that the drive to do that will have to come from you. No teacher can do more than help in the process. Although going to classes or learning with a rabbi once a week can give you a lot of knowledge over time, to seriously know Torah you need a commitment to learn every day. And that commitment can't only be in the Written Law. To understand Torah, you need the Oral Law as well.

No one ever said it was easy to be a Jew. Many other beliefs don't even have one law, we have two!

But why two? Why isn't one law enough? If we examine the Written Law and Oral Law, we find that they focus on very different necessities for our growth.

THE WRITTEN LAW

The Written Law includes the Chumash, the Five Books of Moses; the Books of the Prophets, *Nevi'im*: and the Writings, *Ketuvim*. Together, they make up the 24 books of the Tanach.

From the Written Law, the Tanach, we learn all the basic principles of Jewish belief. From the Chumash, the Five Books, we learn there is a G-d who created us and loves us. We see that He runs the world. We see that He chose the Jewish people as His people, and gave us His Torah in order to direct us. We can appreciate the goal of the Jewish people, to bring G-d to the world. We see that G-d promises us great benefits if we fulfil this mission, and tells us of heavy consequences if we don't.

From the Prophets, we see how the Jewish people lived with what they were commanded to do. We see G-d's reaction to it, both in word and in actions. We can see His commitment to us, but also see that His commitment includes "tough love" when necessary to get us back on track.

From the Writings, Ketuvim, we appreciate deeper aspects of our relationship to G-d. Tehillim, Psalms, teaches us how to emotionally relate to G-d. The Book of Job teaches us what suffering is about. Each book of the Ketuvim is an advanced course on an idea about life we need to understand.

To know all of the written Torah, you need to know Hebrew. You need to be able to delve into the many commentaries of our Sages that help us to get to the deeper meanings.

But Judaism is not all or nothing. There is a lot you can pick up even without language and textual skills, if you approach it in a consistent way.

For the Written Torah, go through the Five Books with the Art Scroll Chumash, and its commentary. Follow the *parsha* of the week and try to get as much as you can by hearing classes on it, listening to CDs on it, and asking questions of your rabbis.

Read through the rest of Tanach, even without commentary, to become familiar with it. There are English books available to explore more deeply what is going on in Joshua, Judges, the books of Samuel and the books of Kings, and the prophecies of Isaiah and his fellow prophets.

The key to getting more out of it is doing it in an organized way.

Have a plan for what you are going to study. Have a review plan so the information stays in your mind and can be used for living.

Gaining familiarity with the text is a start. To go farther and learn wisdom from the Written Torah, it is important to understand certain principles for how to learn it.

First, take the Torah seriously for what it claims to be, a book from G-d. If the Torah is from G-d, it must be telling you the absolute truth. That doesn't mean you have to instantly "agree" with what you read. It means that if you "disagree," you have two possible choices. Either you didn't understand the Torah correctly (so look deeper), or your understanding of life in that particular area is wrong (so understand why you were wrong and change your world-view).

For example: Let's say that you, along with many people today, are against capital punishment. But the Torah calls for it in many instances. Instead of just rejecting the Torah, or blindly throwing away your previous view, check into it more. If you think that the Torah supports stoning a woman to death for suspected adultery (like they still do in Iran today), you are wrongly understanding the Torah. If you think that it is cruel and barbaric to execute a man or a woman for adultery verified through witnesses, after a warning given in advance before the adultery is committed (which the Torah does say), then you need to rethink your concept of how important the marriage relationship is to human society.

It is perfectly OK, and important to growth, to be able to say: I don't understand this, this doesn't seem morally correct to me. As long as you recognize that G-d is the ultimate source of truth and morality (and therefore you need to understand the Torah better or reexamine your own perceptions), those questions only help you towards better understanding.

If the Torah is from G-d, it must all be relevant to you – even things we don't do today, like sacrifices. Work to understand how you can get from it principles of living that apply to your life.

Look at the people in Torah stories as real. When Abraham bows down to three angels who he thinks are ordinary people, ask yourself: how could a wealthy, powerful, highly respected man put himself in such a subservient position before three ordinary people? Why would he do that? What should we learn from Abraham about how we treat people?

Don't take any of the stories of the Torah as just interesting stories. It is all to teach about living. The story of Adam and Eve and the snake is not a fairy tale. It isn't even there to teach history. It is coming to tell you what the basic mistake of humanity is, so we can avoid repeating it.

Don't take any of it as just written for that time and the way people were back then. Torah principles are principles for all time.

When you know the written Torah well, you can use it as a research tool. Do you want to understand what to look for in a wife or husband? Look up the criteria Abraham and Eliezer set for finding a wife for Isaac, and why Rebecca agreed to go with Eliezer to marry Isaac. Do you want to understand the modern world better? Look at the story of Yishmael, the ancestor of the Arabs, to understand the relationship between the Arabs and the Jews. Look at the story of the Tower of Babel to understand what we can expect from the UN.

Way · 15

Accessing the Oral Law

The Written Torah gives us the big picture. That is important. Human beings need to know what the purpose of life is and where they fit in. What it doesn't do is tell us how we can live with our purpose in this world, from day to day, month to month, year to year.

From the Written Torah, we learn we have to keep Shabbat, and how important it is, but not how to keep Shabbat. Only the Oral Law tells us how to do that. From the Oral Law, we learn what constitutes *tefillin*, how to kosher-slaughter animals, that the *esrog* is the beautiful fruit we are commanded to pick up on Sukkot, and the details of every other mitzvah.

Knowing what to do to put the Torah into effect is crucial to being able to live according to G-d's plan. Understanding the purpose of life is necessary, but only when that purpose is reflected in concrete actions does the body feel the need to change. That is why other religions like Christianity and Islam that came out of Judaism adopted many of the big-picture ideas about G-d from the Written Torah, but didn't want the mitzvot of the Oral Law. They liked the philosophy, but they didn't want to change.

The Oral Law had to be much vaster than the Written Law, because all the daily aspects of our lives are much more extensive than the ideas that motivate our actions. In addition, although fundamental principles don't change, they need to be applied in different circumstances. For example, we know from the Written Law that murder is wrong, but is brain-death death? Are you killing someone if you turn off a respirator? When you turn on an electric light that was only invented one hundred years ago, are you violating the laws of Shabbat?

These and many other issues need to be dealt with in the Oral

Law. Not only that, but we lose some clarity in every generation that we don't bring *Mashiach*. We need our Sages to intervene and create the rabbinic laws that help us deal with that decline. Those laws also become part of the Oral Torah.

Because of all this, the task of knowing the Oral Torah is immense. It involves knowing a Talmud that takes 7 years to learn superficially doing a page every day. It involves four sections of the Shulchan Aruch with its commentaries. It involves learning a whole other language besides Hebrew, the Aramaic of the Talmud.

But Rabbi Tarfon, in Pirke Avos, says "It is not upon you to finish the work, but you aren't free to excuse yourself from it." He was speaking about the Oral Law, not the much less extensive Written Law which can be more easily known by every Jew.

We need to start by making a plan how we can learn the Oral Torah, even though we may never finish. It isn't the same plan for everybody. Some people can do Daf Yomi, learning a page of Talmud per day, from the Art Scroll, some can do Mishna. The Dirshu program, a consistent way to master Jewish law, is popular in Jewish communities, and a few minutes every day adds up to a tremendous amount over a few years. You can study the Rambam's Mishne Torah, now in a good English translation with a commentary. Or you can read through all the mitzvot in the Sefer Chinuch in translation. Or study Pirke Avos in the many books available.

Since the Oral Law is the interface of your beliefs and your actions, any action you do based on the Oral Law will change you as a person. In addition, you can use it as a research tool to expand your understanding of an issue. The Oral Law teaches you how to get *shalom bayit*, a better relationship between husband and wife. It teaches how to run your business honestly and what to avoid, how far you can go to save your life and when you have to die for what you believe in, and even how to decide that the *Mashiach* is here when he arrives.

We all feel great respect for an older person from the pre-computer age who is able to master and use successfully the latest modern IT technology. It is hard to develop a new talent. Even many people who have learned in *yeshivot* have deficiencies in their knowledge of Chumash and the rest of Tanach. If we are *ba'alei teshuva*, who returned to Judaism when we were already adults, we are starting out behind. All of us have many other responsibilities that make it difficult for us to take the time to learn the skills of Torah learning. But when something is important, we can make the effort at any age, and nothing is more important than being able to access the wisdom that G-d wants so much to give us.

The work is endless, the possibilities for growth are immense. May we know as much of our two Torahs as we can, and may it continue to add meaning to our lives.

Way · 16

Minimize Business (But Learn from it also)

❡ Don't get overly involved in doing business and making money. Life is about spiritual growth, not the physical satisfactions that come from what money can buy.

❡ G-d created a world where human beings need to work to make a living. The capitalist profit motive is a powerful drive that can be used for good.

❡ Use the lessons from business to learn how to seek spiritual growth in a serious way. King Solomon said: "if you seek it like money, then you can understand the fear of G-d."

❡ Be goal-oriented, efficient, creative, willing to work hard at understanding life, like a businessman does in developing his business.

❡ Use the technique of "borer heshbon," making financial calculations of profit and loss, to see if your life is going in the right direction.

The Hebrew term for Way #16 is *Mi'ut Schorah*, meaning "Minimize Business." This section begins a series of Ways that deal with the physical world and how we can use it and misuse it.

In the world today, the number one meaning for most people is the job they do. They identify themselves as doctor, lawyer, actuary or accountant.

In Jewish philosophy, it isn't like that. Working for a living is a necessity, but it is really a curse. Because Adam ate from the Tree of Knowledge of Good and Evil in the Garden of Eden, G-d said "by the sweat of your brow you will eat bread." Instead of a world where sustenance was available without effort, people would have to struggle to put bread on the table. Instead of a world where people could spend all their time on learning, growing, developing deeper relationships with G-d and other human beings, they would have to spend 40, or 60, or 80 hours a week just ensuring that they could eat.

Because work isn't the ideal, the Rabbis say to "minimize business." Don't treat making money, even though it is a necessity for living, as your life goal. Limit the time you spend at work to the time necessary to make the money you need in order to live. Spend the rest of your time on doing things that bring you closer to the Almighty.

But there is another important tool for living that the Rabbis are indicating when they say "minimize business." They say limit business, don't do away with it entirely. That isn't just because most people need to work to live. Even the person who is independently wealthy, and doesn't have to work, needs to gain something from business.

This is implicit in the story of the Garden of Eden also. The Almighty doesn't punish His children. When we do something wrong, He gives us a means to fix up our mistake. Adam made a mistake, and work was a way to give him and his children what they would need to get back on the right path.

Work fixes up the inability to control our desires, the taking the easy way out, that was a major cause of the first sin. The capitalistic profit motive pushes us to discipline ourselves and use our powers to the utmost. In the book of Proverbs, King Solomon tells us that we need to harness that power: "If you seek it like money," Solomon says, "then you can understand the fear of G-d."

Among the many things we can gain from business experience:

We learn to have a plan. Every business has to be based on a plan, and successful businesses plan for what is ahead. For life we should also have a plan – what growth do we want to achieve? Over what time period? How do we intend to achieve that?

We learn to work efficiently. A businessman schedules his time, and doesn't waste it. He knows he has a limited amount of time in the day to accomplish what he needs to do, and plans accordingly. To achieve something in life, you also should schedule your day and use your time efficiently.

We learn to have priorities. A businessman will cancel his other meetings if he has an important meeting coming up the next day that he has to prepare for. We need to decide what our priorities are between family, Torah learning, helping the community, and working to support our families. We need to make sure that we make enough time for our top priorities.

We learn to be consistent and disciplined. A businessman doesn't sleep late and miss an important meeting. A storekeeper doesn't close down his store because he has a mild illness or headache. If your learning is important to you, be as consistent and disciplined as those businesspeople.

Because of the money we expect to make in the future, we put in years of university without receiving any salary. We apprentice at jobs at low pay. We study things we don't enjoy because we know they are important for our future job. We learn from people we don't necessarily relate to if they can help us to make that money. For our growth in Torah, we should be willing to spend some time in yeshiva if possible, study things that may initially seem uninteresting or difficult to us, learn from people who have what to teach but aren't exciting teachers.

The point of work is that it forces us to be realistic. A businessman has to know what he wants and how he is going to get it done. We need to run our lives with the same realism.

The Rabbis used a financial metaphor to explain to us how to get clear about our lives. They said *borar heshbon*, make a calculation of the reward of a mitzvah vs. the loss from doing it, and the loss from a sin vs. the reward it gives you. Keep books on your life. Are you making a profit or losing out?

The Rabbis didn't want you to spend your whole life just working. They said in Pirke Avos: "limit your work, and work in Torah." But they meant that you should work for your spiritual growth with the same drive that you put into working for the growth of your finances. Only then will your life show the profit that your business shows.

Way · 17

Minimize *Derech Eretz* (But Learn from it also)

- The relationship between a man and a woman is one of the most important relationships we have for learning about our relationship with G-d.

- Sex is the transcendental pleasure that unites the soul and the body in a union that models the transcendental relationship between human beings and the Almighty.

- This transcendental pleasure can only be fully experienced within marriage. Sex without love and commitment turns giving into taking, and is destructive to our spiritual growth.

- By minimizing – utilizing it in the right situation, staying away from it in the wrong situation – we can appreciate its transcendental power.

- The sex drive, with its power of transcendence, teaches us that life can be a transcendental experience.

Way #17 is called "Minimize *Derech Eretz*." Although *derech eretz*, literally "the way of the land," can mean a number of things, here it means "sexual relations." The Rabbis are telling us that we need to harness the power of sex for living.

People who have not studied Talmud may be surprised that the Rabbis talk so openly about sex. But the Sages understood that such a powerful body drive must be crucial to human experience. To understand how to use it and how not to use it must play a special role in the ability of human beings to make the most out of living. "Song of Songs," a book from King Solomon, uses the relationship between a man and a woman as a metaphor for the relationship between G-d and the Jewish people. The Sages included it as one of the holy books of Judaism. They even called it "the holy of holies."

All our relationships, according to Kabbala, teach us something about our relationship to G-d. We learn, through relationship with our parents, that we have a G-d who loves us like a parent and has full commitment to take care of us.

The relationship of a man to a woman also teaches us about our relationship with G-d. The longing of a man for a woman and a woman for a man teaches us about our transcendental longing for a relationship with G-d. "I am sick with love," says one of the lovers in Song of Songs. That the physical relationship between a man and a woman is the greatest of physical pleasures tells us that the transcendental connection between G-d and us is the greatest of all pleasures.

Since the relationship between a man and a woman is so powerful, it has more "do's" and "don'ts" (positive and negative commands) connected with it than almost any other aspect of the Torah.

The most powerful of these positive commands is, "get married." The power of the man-woman relationship to connect you to G-d is only within a totally committed relationship. In marriage, two souls become one, and a person breaks out of his own limitations to truly consider another person. By being able to consider another person, it is possible to get out of selfishness and join together with the Almighty. Without the commitment that marriage involves, people always remain closed up within themselves, and can't totally experience a relationship with G-d.

The second most powerful positive command is to have sexual relations within a marriage relationship. Within marriage, the marital relationship brings the soul and the body together in the most powerful bond. It is the chance for the soul and body together to experience a transcendental experience that models the experience of a human being in a true transcendental union with G-d.

It is this physical version of the transcendental experience that is unique and explains why G-d set up marriage in this way. There is no other experience we have in our daily lives where the body and the soul so experience the working together for the same goal that is the ultimate goal of life. The results of it – greater love between man and wife, the creation of children – testify to the power of creativity that G-d gives the unique human combination of soul and body when they are working together.

The most powerful "don't" of these laws is "don't do it outside of marriage." Our strongest physical drive, when it is separated from commitment, turns something that represents the ultimate in self-lessness and unity into an act of selfishness. And commitment is only possible in a permanent relationship. Temporary relationships, which are becoming the norm in today's society, send a message to both parties that commitment doesn't matter. The separation of such a powerful drive from the total commitment of marriage has led to the increasing decline of marriage and family so evident today in the non-observant world.

Because the drive is so powerful, there are many other "don'ts" connected with it. Don't think about it, dream about it, and read about it. In the religious community, men and women are careful about being alone in friendly relationships with people they aren't married to. Dress codes are set up to keep people from being unnec-essarily attracted to anyone except their spouse. Being careful with the internet is just common sense.

In today's society, these rules are looked at as the height of fanat-icism. When Mike Pence, the Vice President of the U.S., who is an evangelical Christian, mentioned recently that he has rules about having business meetings alone with women other than his wife, and that he doesn't drink at parties when he is alone without his wife, he was criticized for being out of touch and against women. But orthodox Jews would look at these sensible personal restrictions he set for himself as showing how much he cared for his marriage.

The Rabbis expressed all these ideas in the few short words "Minimize Derech Eretz." Don't be overly involved in it. But don't go to the other side and cut it out of your life. By minimizing it, keeping it under strict limits, you can appreciate and harness its incredible power for the transcendental purpose it has.

The High Priest couldn't go whenever he wanted into the Holy of Holies in the Temple. When he did go, on Yom Kippur, it was certainly the highest spiritual experience he would ever have. The heaviest experiences need the greatest protection. The sanctification of marital relations requires the most restraints to preserve it.

Way · 18

Minimize Physical Pleasure
(But Learn from it also)

- ¶ Physical pleasure is positive. Through it, G-d teaches us that the world is good and life is pleasure.

- ¶ Too much focus on physical pleasure prevents us from seeking out higher types of pleasure.

- ¶ The key to using physical pleasure in the right way is to be disciplined. Only use it when you have a positive purpose for doing it.

- ¶ The highest positive purpose for physical pleasure is to achieve spiritual goals.

- ¶ Food is to the body as wisdom is to the soul. Different types of food help us appreciate the benefits of different types of wisdom.

The previous Way, "Minimize *Derech Eretz*," focused on what we can learn from the physical pleasure involved in the relationship of men and women. Way #18– "Minimize Physical Pleasure" (*Mi'ut Taanug* in Hebrew), must be about other physical pleasures. The primary one of these is the pleasure of food, but it applies to other physical pleasures, like going to the beach, wearing nice clothes, having a fast car, exercise, and so much more.

As everyone with even a little knowledge of Judaism knows, we aren't against physical pleasure. We say that G-d created us to have pleasure. The ultimate pleasure is pleasure in G-d, but physical pleasure is also valuable, and serves as a taste of and a pathway to that ultimate pleasure.

Although physical pleasure is good for us, the Rabbis say to "minimize physical pleasure." They mean you should use it where it is good for you, avoid misusing it, and appreciate its value through being disciplined in how you use it.

Most of us have gone on diets on occasion, and many of us use health food. But few people can be on diets all their lives, and there are times when there is a positive reason to eat non-healthy food. What is the central principle that determines what you eat, and whether you should be eating it?

The key to proper use of physical pleasure is to ask yourself: why am I eating now? Is it because I'm hungry? Do I need the energy? Is it because I need to eat to be healthy, and I will get sick if I don't eat regularly? Or is it because I'm bored? Or because I love sweet things, and this is sweet? Or because I am feeling down, and this will cheer me up? Or just because it is time to eat, and I am used to eating at this time?

At first, you don't have to make changes in what you eat. You just want to become aware of your motivations. After that, you can make decisions. Do I really need to eat at this time? Is that piece of cake really going to do something for me? By following through on your decisions, you make your use of the world much more disciplined.

When you start to work on disciplining your eating habits, realize that it isn't going to be easy. Every physical pleasure can become habit-forming, and habits are hard to break. When you try to break one, your body will tell you that it can't stay alive or productive without that particular pleasure. But if you stand up to your body, it will eventually give up.

The basic principle for this discipline is: if it isn't needed, don't do it. If it will have a positive result, do it. When you have had enough, stop.

It isn't enough to eat just to be healthy, have energy, or feel good about the world. The Rabbis say in Pirke Avos, "all your actions should be for the sake of Heaven." They meant that all your actions – including eating and taking other physical pleasures – should be for a spiritual goal. Even when you are hungry, and it is healthy for you to eat, don't eat just because it's healthy. Eat because you want to be healthy so you can accomplish something for G-d, to learn better, do His mitzvot better, and help His people better.

Physical pleasure is only one type of the pleasures that G-d created. There are five levels of pleasure in this world – physical pleasure, love, the pleasure of being good, the pleasure of being creative, and the pleasure of connecting with G-d. (We discuss aspects of each throughout the 48 Ways). Physical pleasure is the lowest level. But it is the foundation for all the other pleasures, because it is the most easily available. It teaches us that G-d's world is good and that life is pleasure. It gives us spiritual energy that we can use to go after the higher pleasures.

Therefore, even though you should have a spiritual purpose in mind when you are taking physical pleasure, don't forget that it is a mitzvah to appreciate the pleasure! That is why we say a blessing before we eat something. We focus on the fact that G-d provided this world of pleasure for my own good.

On a deeper level, there is a kabbalistic meaning to food. The Rabbis say that food is to the body as wisdom is to the soul. Halacha, Jewish law, is like bread, because it provides the basic structure a person needs. The discussions of the Talmud are like meat, because they give strength to the mind like meat gives strength to the body. Kabbala is like wine, because it gives you an access to deeper understandings about existence like wine gives you access to deeper feelings.

Although physical pleasures are powerful and positive, the Rabbis say to minimize them. Too much material pleasure can be an escape, a way to avoid the effort of going after the higher pleasures. But if you have the discipline to use only what you need, your physical pleasures become the stepping stone to your higher goals.

Way · 19

Minimize Sleep (But Learn from it also)

❧ The Rabbis say that sleep is 1/60th of death. When you are sleeping, you aren't living. So cut down on unnecessary sleep.

❧ Minimize, but don't overdo it. Get the sleep that is necessary for your health.

❧ How can you tell what is necessary? Become aware of how much you sleep normally and try not to do more than that.

❧ Take opportunities to fight sleep, especially when learning Torah.

❧ The positive power of sleep is to appreciate how it feels to wake up. When we fall asleep to life, growth, change, wisdom, we need to practice waking ourselves up. Life provides tremendous opportunities – wake up to those opportunities.

Way #19 – "Minimize Sleep," (*Mi'ut Shaina* in Hebrew) deals with another one of the physical pleasures, sleeping. Like the last few ways, "minimize" means: there is a way to use it positively, but don't do it too much.

Sleep is a need of all human beings. But why did an Almighty Creator make it necessary for His creations to sleep? If the world was just a result of random evolution, we can understand that sleep was just a glitch in the machine. But we don't believe that. So why would G-d, who created us to get the most out of life, have us spend almost a third of that life sleeping? A machine has the capacity to run without resting – why couldn't G-d give us that capability?

Because sleep seems so opposite to the purpose of living, the Rabbis said to minimize it to the extent that we can. They said "sleep is 1/60th of death," and the Torah says: choose life.

But sleep is a physical need in order to be effective, so we need to be careful about how we minimize it.

First, just be aware of how much you are sleeping. Do you need as much as you are getting?

If your sleeping patterns vary, do what you can to make them regular. Obviously, this doesn't apply to parents of small children. But if you are able to set a pattern for yourself, make a decision not to sleep more than your average. Except on rare occasions don't "sleep in" on Sundays and holidays. Just because you have the opportunity to sleep more, you don't necessarily need to use it.

Once you have a regular sleep time, whether it is six or eight hours a day, experiment with lowering it. Do small amounts at a time. Lowering your usual sleep requirements five minutes a day gives you 35 minutes extra life a week, more than 30 hours a year.

Be sensitive to what you need, and don't over-minimize. When I was a student at Aish Hatorah in Jerusalem, I became aware of the *frum yetzer hara*. People would hear Rabbi Weinberg teach this class and decide they could get by on 4 hours of sleep. After a few weeks, they were sick in bed and had a lot of time to sleep.

Develop the consciousness that fighting sleep is fighting for life. Don't just turn off and stop learning because you're tired. If you were tired and suddenly you heard the Super Bowl was playing, you would wake yourself up. You can learn to wake yourself up without the Super Bowl. Turn on joy (Way #8, "Living with Joy"). Focus on what is deep and meaningful in what you are learning. Or just stand up. Sometimes, putting your head down and taking a five-minute nap will enable you to go another few hours.

In yeshivot, they have "*mishmar* night" on Thursday when students stay up all night to learn that they can fight sleep. On Shavuot night, we fight sleep to teach ourselves just how important the Torah is.

Rav Noach used to say that his father, a businessman, would never sleep in a bed except on Shabbos. He would fall asleep while learning and wake up and continue learning.

Fighting sleep is fighting death. But we still need to answer the question: why would G-d make sleep a necessity for His creations?

The reason is that sleep, like everything that G-d created, has an immensely positive purpose.

In physical terms, that positive purpose is to refresh the body and mind. When we are tired, we don't think clearly, we don't have the energy to do things. We go to sleep and wake up and we are new people. We think more clearly, we have the energy to accomplish in the day.

Of course, G-d didn't have to create us to get tired like that. The physical tiredness is just to teach us about spiritual tiredness. After spending time on learning or other spiritual growth accomplishments, we get tired of them. We get tired of trying to learn new things. We get tired of trying to develop our relationships with the people close to us. If we are committed to a cause, we get tired of the fact that progress is so slow. We get tired of having to say the same daily prayer every day.

Going to sleep and waking up refreshed teaches us that we can wake up in living also. Wake up and look at the Torah portion of the week as if it was new. Wake up and look at your wife/ husband. Wake up and rethink your cause. Wake up and refocus your davening.

Teshuva is the spiritual waking up from the spiritual sleep we fall into. The Rambam says that the shofar on Rosh Hashana has the purpose to wake up everyone who has been spiritually sleeping all year.

So sleep as little as you can get by with. The less sleep, the more life. But when you do sleep, pay attention to the pleasure of waking up. Use that pleasure to wake you up to the tremendous potential of life.

Way · 20

Minimize Conversation
(But Learn from it also)

¶ Conversation, "sicha," is casual conversation about life events, not deep discussions about life and meaning.

¶ Conversation is a desire of the body. Like all desires of the body, it can be used properly or misused.

¶ Improper use of conversation is to discuss trivialities that add nothing to your understanding of life. Even worse is to use conversation to talk about other people.

¶ Proper use of conversation is to use it to get at the wisdom and aspirations of other human beings, so you can learn from them and help them.

¶ Ask other people about their goals and life experiences. Instead of telling them about yourself, learn about them.

When you walk into certain synagogues, you hear a buzz. Unfortunately, it isn't the buzz of people praying to connect to their Creator. It's the buzz of people getting together and sharing what has been going on with them during the week.

The drive people have to communicate with each other while praying can't only be a soul drive, one soul reaching out to connect with another. It must be that the body has a strong drive to connect with others also. Like every physical drive, it has a positive purpose and it can be misused. The Rabbis teach, in Way #20, (*Mi'ut Sicha* in Hebrew) that we should "Minimize conversation." Use it when it is positive, cut it out when it is negative.

The "conversation" we are talking about isn't discussions about Torah learning or heart-to-heart talks about your direction in life. Those are obvious soul needs. The conversations this Way is referring to are the ones you have about how things are going at work, how your kids are doing at school, what exercise you are doing at gym, why Trump is going to save the world or mess up the world, and many other subjects. What purpose do these conversations serve?

In fact, every conversation can be used to gain insight into the hidden world of other human beings. All of us have experiences in life, deeper perceptions, ideals and goals that we don't generally reveal to anyone who isn't very close to us. Conversation is a way to get at those hidden facets of human experience and the lessons on life that other people have learned.

In order to make use of conversation to do this, you have to first appreciate what is negative about the normal conversations we often have. Certainly, to talk in shul about our mortgages is not very productive when we should be talking with G-d about our lives. But even conversations about business or vacations in more neutral settings can be a waste of time. We would think it crazy to see someone throwing money away every few minutes. Time is money, and an unnecessary conversation can use up time worth much more than dollar bills.

In addition, undirected conversation can lead to *loshen hora* – it is even more fun to speak about other people than it is to talk about vacationing in Europe. It can lead to making fun of other people – we and our conversation partner can share a beautiful moment at the expense of someone else. It can lead to us feeling unhappy and dissatisfied and needing to keep up with the Joneses, who have taken the trip to Mauritius we can't afford.

So what can you do? First, make a decision that you don't want conversations about trivialities. If you feel there is no point to the conversation, seek a way to get out of it. "I have to run now" is not being dishonest – there are some people you do have to run away from.

But a better response would be to ask yourself – what do I want to know about this person? What would I want to know about any human being?

93

For example, ask someone: what do you do for your work? That's a good ice-breaker. But follow up. If the person is a lawyer, or a teacher, or a filmmaker, you can find out: what projects are they working on? What interesting things have they seen recently? My father was a policeman in New York for 30 years, and had lots of interesting stories to tell anyone who would think to ask. Ask a teacher: what is it like to be a teacher in a Jewish school, or to be white in a school that is mostly black?

Sometimes you can get deeper insights by asking a person what he would like to do, instead of what he is doing. Ask a new mother if motherhood has changed what she thinks about life. Or ask people what problems they have had, and how have they dealt with them?

It helps to read a good book about dealing with people, like Dale Carnegie's How to Win Friends and Influence People. Know the person's name, be interested, learn to listen, and don't tell a person he is wrong are tried and true principles for conversation.

By conversing with people, you can learn a lot of wisdom, because every person is different and each has his own world. They don't always know how to directly share it with you, but if you talk with them you can access many of their insights. And knowing what people are thinking is the first step to being able to love them and help them, and even to know how they can help you.

Included in the idea of "minimize conversation" is the idea of minimizing your words when you are in a conversation. Say what has to be said in the most concise way. The Rabbis say "the words of the wise are few and their meanings are many."

In contrast, if a person talks too much, people judge he has nothing to say.

May we succeed in communicating with people in the right way at the right time. And when we are in shul, just have a conversation with G-d.

Minimize Laughter (But Learn from it also)

§ Laughter is a pleasurable release of tension. If used in the right way, it gives you energy for living. Used in the wrong way, it can be an excuse to avoid living.

§ Using it in the right way means to contrast our sense of self-importance with the reality of our existence. We make fun of unrealistic ideas and expectations.

§ It is also using it the right way to make fun of wrong and dangerous ideas.

§ The wrong way to use laughter is to make fun of other people or of valuable and meaningful ideas.

§ A good teacher uses laughter to relax his audience before getting serious.

The late unlamented dictator and spiritual leader of Iran, Ayatollah Khomeini, once said: there are no jokes in Islam. He meant that Islam is a very serious religion, with many requirements and responsibilities to a G-d who gives immense rewards and punishments. Nothing to laugh about there! And we see that Islamic fundamentalist terrorists don't have much of a sense of humor. Even if their religion allowed it, you probably wouldn't enjoy going out with them for a beer.

Judaism is also a very serious religion, with many requirements and responsibilities to a G-d who gives immense rewards and punishments. But when the Rabbis say, in Way #21 – "Minimize laughter" (*Mi'ut S'chok* in Hebrew), they are telling us that laughter has a place in Judaism. Like all the previous "Minimizes," they are telling us that we shouldn't overdo it – but used in the right way, it is not only good to laugh, but necessary for living. And Jews have internalized the pleasure of laughter. As international speaker Ken Spiro pointed out, if the percentage of famous Jewish comedians compared to non-Jewish comedians were indicative of the amount of Jews in the world, there would be a billion Jews.

To understand why laughter and jokes are pleasurable, and why they are important for living, we need to understand what makes a joke a joke.

Many years ago, I read a book called "The Act of Creation" by the Jewish writer and philosopher Arthur Koestler. The main thing I remember from it was his analysis of what makes a joke funny.

Every joke, he said, was the coming together of two conflicting views of reality. When Groucho Marx said "these are my principles, and if you don't like them I have others," the joke was about the contradiction between an upright man living with principles, which are absolute and unchanging, and a dishonest person who is ready to change any of his principles in order to make a deal. When the comedian W.C. Fields said "I remember the day I spent a month in Philadelphia," the contrast between a short day and a long month told us how boring Philadelphia was. The deflating of one seeming reality by another causes a pleasurable release of tension that we recognize as laughter.

Once we understand what a joke is we can understand why laughter is important for us and how it can be misused.

On the simplest level, because laughter is a pleasurable release of tension, a good teacher often starts with a joke, because it makes people ready to listen. The Talmud says that the great teacher Rav would do it, and all the best Jewish speakers today do it.

But on a deeper level, what makes a joke a proper use of humor or a negative one is based on what views of reality you are contrasting.

What is a worthwhile joke? It often involves contrasting our exaggerated sense of self-importance with reality. In old slapstick movies, it would be the pompous man who slips on a banana peel. In Jewish jokes, it would be Goldberg, who is mad at G-d for not listening to his many prayers to win the lottery, until G-d tells him: "Goldberg, help Me out, just buy a ticket!" That joke applies to a lot of us who expect G-d to take care of us like Goldberg, but don't want to make the efforts we could make.

When we laugh at ourselves, we can enjoy life more and don't necessarily need to feel that we are owed everything by everybody. We can recognize that we are responsible for our failings, and have renewed energy to do something about it.

Laughter is also useful when we laugh by taking false ideas and contrasting them to reality. At Mount Carmel, the prophet Eliyahu made fun of the false god Baal by asking its followers whether the Baal isn't listening to them because he is going to the bathroom. For the Jews at the time, who were drawn to worship of the Baal, it was important to hear the Baal being ridiculed.

In the same way, we make jokes about the idols and false philosophies of today. Margaret Thatcher famously said: "the problem with socialism is that sooner or later you run out of other people's money." Jokes can point out the craziness of the terrorist death cult ("the kids blow up so fast"), or the mistaken social ideas of Western society. It makes us realize how confused the world we are living in is, so that we don't get caught up in it.

When is a joke used in the wrong way? When it makes fun of concepts that are true and meaningful. Jokes about marriage comparing marriage to a prison sentence don't make marriages stronger. Jokes about extra-marital affairs and sexual immorality, like so many modern comedians specialize in, weaken the social restrictions that ultimately maintain marriage and family. Jokes about people who take religion to the extreme can be good, because they make fun of rigidity and too much self-importance. But jokes about keeping Jewish law or maintaining Jewish values can destroy very important laws and values.

The worst types of jokes are those that ridicule people. Although friendly jokes can be used to help people relax and see themselves more clearly, jokes aimed at making fun of people can be deeply hurtful. Even when they are based on mistakes the person is making or bad character flaws, ridicule isn't justified. Faults aren't the essence of a person, and ridicule makes it seem like they are.

Laughter can also often be used by people to avoid dealing with important issues. Don't laugh off legitimate criticism. *Laitzanut,* making fun of everything, sets up a wall against anyone telling you the mistakes you are making or teaching you new ideas.

G-d and the purpose of life, good and evil, are serious issues, and you can't take them lightly. But a person who carries around too much seriousness and self-importance will be too burdened down to accomplish much. When you can laugh at your limitations, it can give you the energy to change your life and the world.

Way · 22

Conquering Anger and Frustration

❡ Learning how to conquer anger is necessary to leading a good life. The Sages say that the life of an angry person is not a life.

❡ The way to fight anger in most situations is to realize that there is nothing to be angry about. People make mistakes. And even when it is right to be angry, when something really wrong has been done, it is often better to fake anger rather than actually feel it.

❡ Frustration is a type of anger. Frustration at the difficulties of carrying out what we decide causes us to give up on many important goals. Giving up causes us to develop a credibility gap within ourselves.

❡ The first step to dealing with frustration is to commit yourself to carry through on your decisions, even if they are harder to carry out than you thought they would be.

❡ Keep struggling with the frustrations of understanding what you are living for, and frustrations with progress in Torah learning. Don't give up.

Anger is one of our most dangerous, counter-productive emotions. The Rabbis say "the life of an angry person is not a life." They say "Anyone who gets angry, it is as if he is worshipping idols." Angry abusive husbands or angry abusive wives can make life unbearable and marriage impossible.

Frustration is a quieter form of anger. When Rav Noach taught this Way, *"erech apayim"* in Hebrew – "Be slow to anger" – he focused more on fighting frustration. While most people are aware of the dangers of anger, and at least make some effort to control it, frustration and its negative effects are much less appreciated.

To understand emotions, it's necessary to understand the perceptions that cause them. Anger results from the perception that something wrong has been done. That person is driving too slowly – he should know better! My husband stayed late at work without telling me – he's so insensitive! My children don't appreciate that I am tired and stressed out today – that is so selfish of them!

We can deal with anger by realizing that the wrong, if it was done, was excusable. Every driver has times when he or she isn't paying attention – you may even have driven too slowly yourself on occasion. Every husband has times when he forgets to call his wife – sometimes the wife even forgets to call him. Kids are by nature disruptive and unfeeling – that is why G-d forced them to have parents.

There are times when anger can be justified. Anger is a legitimate response to a real evil. Be angry at anti-Semites, especially Jewish ones, who attack Israel and support boycotts. But because anger is such a powerful and dangerous emotion, the Rabbis say you shouldn't be angry even in most situations where anger is justified. Fake anger with your children when they do something wrong, but don't get really angry.

Frustration is also anger. It can be passive anger directed at someone else, when you feel they are doing something wrong but don't want to lash out at them. More often, it is anger directed at yourself – I'm not accomplishing what I should be accomplishing, I am stuck in a dead-end job and I am too afraid to get out of it. Or it can be directed at G-d or the world---life is just too tough, I can't take doing this anymore.

You can see the negative effect of frustration if you look at all those things you wanted to do that you gave up on because you got frustrated. You started a diet and you gave up because progress was so slow. You started going to minyan in the morning, and hit a few tough days when you slept in, and you gave up. You wanted to learn Hebrew, enrolled in a course, didn't do the homework, and quit. You wanted to spend more time with your kids, but you got frustrated at them when they weren't immediately responsive.

In all these cases, you didn't stop because the goal was unrealistic. But it was difficult, and progress wasn't immediate. In the short term, it was just too frustrating.

The immediate results were not losing weight, not getting to minyan, not knowing Hebrew, or not improving your relationship with your kids. But when you give up on something you have decided to do, it causes something even worse. It creates a credibility gap in yourself. You don't believe you can make a decision and really change. How can you be motivated to make real changes on Yom Kippur this year when you didn't follow through on your decisions the previous Yom Kippur?

So when you make a decision, decide you will carry through with it, even if it is difficult. Even if it is more difficult than you thought. You will gain credibility with yourself if you know you can live with what you decide.

Since this isn't easy, don't do too many things at once. Make advances one step at a time. Commit yourself to going to minyan for one month. After you've done that, commit yourself to take one extra step in learning. As you see you can do it, you will grow in confidence.

Obviously there will be times when you make a decision to do something that is really beyond your abilities. But be clear that it is really too much for you before you stop it. In Path of the Just, Rabbi Moshe Chaim Luzzatto sets down a principle: "all easy ways need to be examined." Our body tries to avoid pain, so be careful of the rationalization that you are in over your head.

The easiest frustrations to deal with are the ones involving actions – to spend more time learning, to learn Hebrew, to go to minyan. The deeper frustrations in life involve the deeper aspects: how do I work out what I am really living for, how can I learn to really take joy in life, how can I really use my unique potential, how can I improve my marriage?

With all these, the basic principle is not to give up making the effort. In Proverbs, it says "A righteous person falls seven times and gets up." So even a righteous person falls down, but he doesn't give up.

Although you need to fight frustration to achieve goals, frustration can also be lowered by positive thinking. Our frustration with how hard G-d sometimes seems to make life can be dealt with by thinking about the great reward we get from dealing with hardship. Our frustration with our own lack of progress can be dealt with by focusing on how much we have accomplished and how much good we already have in our lives. Our frustrations with other people can be countered by appreciating their virtues and that we love them and care about them.

Rabbi Noach Weinberg named Aish Hatorah "the fire of Torah" based on a story in the Midrash about the great Rabbi Akiva and how he dealt with frustration. Rabbi Akiva was 40 years old and unlearned. One day he saw a stone in a river that had a hole that had been hollowed out by the running water. He said: If water can make a hole in a stone, surely Torah, which is like fire, can get through to my heart.

Rav Noach asked: what did Rabbi Akiva see about the stone that made such a deep impression? He answered: Rabbi Akiva wasn't someone who had never tried to learn Torah. He tried, but he didn't see it changing him, so he gave up. When he saw the stone, he realized: each drop of water on the stone doesn't seem to have any effect, yet somehow the water makes a hole in the stone. Torah, if I keep with it, will certainly have an effect on my heart.

May we all commit ourselves to being changed by the Fire of Torah, and not give up even if we don't see immediate results.

Way · 23

Being a Good Person: Having a Good Heart

- ¶ One of the strongest desires of a human being is to be good. Not only the soul wants to be good, so does the body. That is why human beings are willing to die to be good, even people we would normally think of as evil, such as terrorists who kill innocent civilians in suicide bombings.

- ¶ "Choosing good" means choosing what the soul "wants" rather than what the body "feels like." In the Torah, it is described as "choosing life."

- ¶ The angel taught us what is good along with the rest of the Torah. The fact that human beings have so much difficulty agreeing about what is good is because of the negative desires of the body, and the ability of the yetzer hara to argue that following those desires is really "good."

- ¶ The bottom-line quality of a good person is the willingness to seek the truth, live with what is true, and change when he or she discovers his or her mistakes.

- ¶ Greatness comes from combining the desire of the soul and the body to be good.

One of the strongest desires of human beings is to be a good person. That is why Way #23 – "Being a Good Person: Having a Good Heart" (*Lev Tov* in Hebrew) is such a powerful tool for living. Every human being is a spiritual soul. The soul wants to connect with G-d. It wants to live with truth, do the right thing, and have meaningful accomplishments. That's why Judaism's answer to the question "are human beings basically good" is yes, because the soul wants only good.

But our souls are connected to our bodies, and the body has many desires: for comfort, for physical gratification, for ego gratification. The free will struggle in human beings is for the soul to control and direct the body, and it is a tough and challenging battle.

But the drives of the body are not all negative. The soul has a powerful ally, the drive of the body to be good. This is called "a good heart," because in Jewish understanding the heart is the seat of emotions.

The proof of the power of this drive is that we are all willing to die for it. A suicide bomber is dying to be good, according to his concept. All of us would have something we could not do – kill 100 children, betray our family – even if we would be killed if we didn't. We know that we couldn't think of ourselves as good people if we gave in to save our lives.

You can see it in yourself if you ask yourself: If you had to choose, would you be happy, wise or good? No one could honestly answer that they would rather be a happy but evil person or a wise but evil person.

If you feel you aren't good, it eats away at you. Even evil people have to find a way to rationalize that they are good. My father was a policeman in New York and told me that they never caught a criminal, even for a terrible crime like child molesting, who didn't have an excuse.

WHAT IS "GOOD"?

Since the drive to be good is so powerful, we need to find a way to use it in living. But first we have to know what "good" is. That isn't so clear. If you ask an evil man or a good man "are you a good man?" the evil man would be more likely to answer that he is a good man. A terrorist, who is doing evil, thinks he is a really good man. The average person in Western society, who isn't doing evil but isn't doing so much good either, thinks he is a good man as long as he isn't actively hurting others.

So what's the definition of "good"? As we mentioned in Way #4 – "Connecting with Your Intuition: Understanding of the Heart," all of us have "wants" and "feel likes." "Wants" are permanent and meaningful – we want wisdom, meaningful relationships, to help people and make the world a better place, to have self-respect. "Feel likes" are transitory and comfortable sensations. We feel like reading escapist literature rather than learning wisdom. We feel like shallow relationships rather than putting in the effort for deeper relationships. We feel like having other people give us respect, even if it isn't based on real accomplishments.

"Wants" are really the drives of the soul, "feel likes" the desires of the body.

The Jewish definition of "good" is to live with what you want to do, not what you feel like doing.

The Torah expresses this definition in a deeper way. In the book of Devarim, Moshe says to the Jewish people "I have placed before you today life and good, death and evil." Then he commands the Jewish people to "choose life." He means to tell us that choosing life over death is choosing good over evil.

But what does that mean? Even an evil person wants to live!

Moshe is telling us to choose our "wants," everything that leads to a meaningful life. Our "feel-likes" represent death on the installment plan. The Rabbis say a righteous person is alive even after he is dead, because he lives on in the World-to-come and his impact lives on after him. They say a wicked person is dead even when he is alive, because he is destroying himself while he is alive.

So being good includes not harming others. But it also includes caring for and helping others. And it also includes learning wisdom, developing a relationship with G-d, taking responsibility for your own actions. Living with these "wants," and fighting the body's desires, which often conflict with these "wants," is choosing "life" and choosing "good."

THE MISTAKE OF THE EVIL MAN
WHO THINKS HE IS GOOD

But what about the evil man who really thinks he is good? The Islamic terrorist thinks that he "wants" to kill the infidel in the name of Islam. Hitler thought he "wanted" to destroy the Jews for the good of humanity.

We have already mentioned in Way #4 – "Connecting with Your Intuition: Understanding of the Heart," the Sages' understanding that an angel taught us all wisdom in the womb. That includes the knowledge of what is good, what contributes to real living and what doesn't. Every human being really knows what is good, and 'good' is an objective reality. The soul, which wants to live with truth, can't 'want' to do evil.

So how does evil get done, and why do evil people, as mentioned, really think they are good?

To understand, let us imagine a conversation between Hitler and an orthodox rabbi.

Hitler: Rabbi X, don't you agree that if there is one group that by its own innate evil nature, which cannot be changed, is destroying life for all the rest of humanity, that group needs to be wiped out?

Rabbi X: I agree with you. That is why the Torah commands us to wipe out the nation of Amalek.

So, with regard to a basic principle of good, Hitler and Rabbi X are in agreement. What makes Hitler an evil man? Only when we get to Hitler's follow-up.

Hitler: Rabbi X, don't you agree that the Jews are that people?

Rabbi X (and I hope most of us) would disagree strongly. The Jews have given the world many of its most fundamental moral teachings and continue to help the world today in many important ways.

So what makes Hitler an evil man? The emotion of hatred that is driving him to twist reality to see the world's most productive people as Amalek, worthy of destruction. That emotion of the body then gets supported by the "*yetzer hara*," "the evil inclination," the lawyer for the body's desire, to seek reasons in the computer viruses the mind has picked up (Jews only care about money, they secretly want to control the world, they hate the Gentiles). Those reasons tell him that the Jews are the world's worst people. Then he can pervert the body's desire to be good and use it to make the intense effort necessary to turn his false concept of good into action.

Since all human beings want to be good, evil can only be done through rationalizing something bad as good. The greater the rationalization, the more a person has to twist reality to rationalize, the greater the evil.

WHO IS A GOOD MAN?

Since the body will always try to rationalize its desires as good, human beings don't find it easy to know how to be good. And even the person who has a clear concept of good will have many moments when he doesn't live up to what he thinks is good. So how do we know if we are good people or not?

The Torah tells us that we are good people if we are willing to make the effort to really seek out truth, to connect with what the angel taught us, and to follow it wherever it leads. It tells us about Joseph's brothers, who are considered the good and righteous ancestors of the Jewish people, even though they misjudged Joseph, wanted to kill him, and sold him as a slave. Why? Because, even though they rationalized that they were right when they planned to kill Joseph (they thought he was a dangerous man, out to destroy them spiritually), they were willing to consider they made a mistake. They wanted to find out, and, when they found out, they were ready to admit it and change.

In contrast, imagine a suicide bomber, who is ready to blow himself up with a bus of women and children based on what he thinks is good. You say to him: "Do you think you are doing the right thing because the Koran said so – how do you know that the Koran is true? Maybe Mohammed was not telling the truth when he said G-d spoke to him." Do you think he is going to say: "That's an interesting question, I never thought of that!" Or, "Here are my proofs that the Koran is true!" It is doubtful that he would do that, and he likely would blow you up for attacking Mohammed. An evil man who thinks he is good has no interest in finding the truth. The emotion that is driving his actions blocks out listening to any conflicting information, whether from his own intuitions or from the world outside.

GOOD TO GREAT

Living to be good involves getting in touch with what the angel taught you, both through learning G-d's Torah (Way #1 – "Life-Long Study") and connecting with your intuition (Way #4 – "Connecting with Your Intuition: Understanding of the Heart"). But "greatness," striving to be good all the time, requires yet another step. It isn't enough to intellectually understand the good that needs to be done, and to force yourself to live by it. To live with good on a constant basis, your body needs to access the emotion of "a good heart."

Once you are focused on following truth, place your emotional drive to be a good person behind it and live with it. Choose life on a constant basis.

Realize that this is your pleasure. Being good is the third of the Five Levels of Pleasure. We would sacrifice physical pleasure, and even the pleasure of love in order to be good (in Way #33 – "Love Doing What's Right," we talk more about this). Although being good is also painful, pain is not the opposite of pleasure, as we will talk about in Way #25 – "Enduring and Accepting Pain."

The role model in Jewish history for doing this is the great Rabbi Akiva. When the Romans ruling over Israel made a decree against public teaching of Torah, Rabbi Akiva went out and taught Torah in public. The Romans took him and sentenced him to execution in public in a particularly cruel and painful way. His students were invited to the execution. They saw that, as he was being tortured, he was saying the Shema. They asked him how he could do that at a time of such painful suffering. He said to them: "All my life, I was pained by the statement in the Torah, 'love G-d with all your soul,' meaning 'even if He takes your soul'. I said: when will I have the opportunity to fulfill this? Now that I have the opportunity, shouldn't I fulfill it?" He died while joyously saying the word "One" in the Shema.

We all have in us the willingness to die to be good, like Rabbi Akiva. We don't look for martyrdom, but if it would happen, like Rabbi Akiva, we should accept it with the joy that Rabbi Akiva had.

But better than dying for G-d is to live for G-d. If something is important enough for you to die for, then it is important enough to live for. If the Jewish people mean enough to you that you would fight in the Israeli army for their survival, live for them and commit yourself to their cause.

Jewish law, prayer, commitment to Torah learning are all testing grounds for using your desire to be good. Appreciate that it is good, choosing life, to keep *halacha*, pray with a *minyan*, or learn something every day. Don't just force yourself to do these things.

Make use of your body's desire to do good to take pleasure in doing them.

Whenever you hear something that is true, fight to understand it. Make it your own, and do something about it. That is the bottom line of being a good person.

Way · 24

Belief in Wise People

¶ Belief (emuna) is based on evidence. To accept something on faith is based on emotion. Judaism says: have emuna, not faith.

¶ Belief in a wise man needs to be based on evidence of his wisdom. To trust in a leader because of his charisma or mystical abilities is faith.

¶ Belief in the wise man is necessary for the many areas of life where you are not sure of the answer. In that case, trust in his answer even when you don't understand it.

¶ If proven wise men testify to the wisdom of someone else, trusting in that "someone else" is also belief, not faith. The wisdom of the Talmud is testified to by all the wise men of the Jewish people, so it deserves trust.

¶ To become great, you need to trust in the extra wisdom of wise people, and to learn from them.

Way #24 is *Emunat Chachamim*, "Belief in Wise People." One of the first things that Rav Noach Weinberg taught us when we were beginners in studying Judaism at Aish Hatorah in Jerusalem, was how to rationally go about examining whether there is a G-d and whether Torah is truly from G-d. He set down four different types of convictions that lead people to accept something as true. It is crucial to understand each one clearly.

The first type of conviction is "Society." Most people believe what they believe because of an accident of birth. If you are born in Iran, you will likely believe what Iranians believe. A Jew born in Mea Shearim will likely believe what his culture believes.

The second type of conviction is "Faith," here defined as an emotional or unreasoned belief. You believe it because you desire to believe it. The many people in the 20th century who believed in Nazism or Communism, philosophies that together led to the deaths of more than 100 million people, did not believe in those philosophies because of convincing evidence of the special superiority of the German people or the utopia that would result from the dictatorship of the proletariat. Those illusions felt good to them, so they decided that they believed in them and would even die for them.

Society and faith are not good reasons to decide what is true. How do you know your society is the right one or that your emotion is more "true" than someone else's emotion?

The third type of conviction is *Emuna*, "belief." It isn't based on emotion, but it isn't based on absolute proof either. It is based on having enough evidence to decide that it is reasonable to act a certain way.

For example, imagine paying with a check (in the ancient days when people still paid with checks). The store owner doesn't say: I have faith in the goodness of human beings, so I will accept everyone's check. He also can't say without knowing you: I know for sure that this check won't bounce. What does he do? He sets standards: Proper identification, do you look like a reliable person, and other standards. Based on that, he can trust, or "believe" that your check is likely to be good, and run his business based on it.

The fourth type of conviction is "Knowledge." It is based on so much evidence that we are sure that it can't be any other way. Warren Buffett's check is not going to bounce.

With regard to the existence of G-d and Torah being true, Judaism says to start with *Emuna* and work toward knowledge. That is why Jewish organizations like Arachim and Aish Hatorah have programs where they give the evidence that leads to belief and then to knowledge.

But the concept of "belief" vs. "faith" applies in other contexts also. This Way says "believe" in wise men.

In Way #10 – "Seeking Wisdom from the Wise," we discussed the need to learn from wise people. Building one's life is more complicated than building a bridge, with a greater chance of failure. As explained earlier, just as we wouldn't think of building a bridge without proper instruction and education in engineering, we also shouldn't think of making major decisions in our lives without consulting wise individuals who can share their knowledge with us.

When a teacher imparts wisdom, we must hear it and judge it. We are responsible before G-d for our own actions, so we can't justify going against what we know by saying "that is what my teacher told me." If there is a way we can judge the validity of the content that our teacher is relaying to us, we need to make that effort to judge.

Way #24 tells us to take a step further in growth. We have to make our own decisions on the things we can understand on our own, but what about the things we don't yet know? What if we don't have enough knowledge to judge one way or the other? Decisions on some of the most important steps we need to take in our lives may be beyond our ability with the limited knowledge that we have.

For example: What school should my children attend? Do I totally understand the issues and long-range consequences of sending them to one school or another? How should I divide my learning time to learn Torah in the most effective way? If I want to do something to help Jews, what is the help that is most needed? Is it giving charity to poor Jews, building day schools to teach Jewishly-connected Jews, outreach to totally unconnected Jews, getting involved with Jewish organizations trying to protect Israel and the Jewish community politically? Or something else entirely?

To the level where you can understand these issues yourself, you should gather your own wisdom. And where you reach the limits of your own understanding and knowledge, the Rabbis say: have belief in the wise man. Listen to what your teacher says even if you don't totally understand it yet or see it for yourself.

That doesn't mean to trust any teacher. Belief is based on evidence. To listen to a teacher because society says he is wise, or because he seems to have mystical powers, is having "faith" in a teacher, not belief.

But if a teacher has already shown you that he has wisdom and he has taught ideas about life that you were able to implement, it makes sense to listen to him about other ideas you aren't so clear about. If a stock market analyst gave you tips on the market that worked, it would make sense to listen to his next tip.

The guiding principle is: the more wisdom you see that a person has, the more credence you can give to his statements even when he doesn't explain himself. Spend more time trying to understand what he is saying. Don't jump to the conclusion that he is wrong or incapable of understanding your issues.

Even when you haven't previously learned from him, if a teacher comes recommended by people whose wisdom you trust, it still makes sense to take his wisdom seriously.

The Sages of the Talmud are the wise teachers that are recommended by all the wise men of Judaism as explained by the many commentaries. A system that has successfully kept the Jewish people going for thousands of years should certainly merit some trust, even when you don't understand all its wisdom.

This also applies to the top Torah scholars of our generation, the rabbis who have been accepted by the most knowledgeable Torah scholars of the Jewish people as their leaders. We take what they say with great seriousness, even when it might seem to us that they are making a mistake.

Only G-d is infallible, and all human beings can make mistakes. G-d still expects you to think for yourself. It is possible that, based on your unique circumstances, you may understand something they don't. But have humility, say "I don't understand why he said that" rather than "He's wrong."

GREAT PEOPLE CAN TEACH YOU HOW TO BE GREAT

What I have presented above is what Rabbi Noach Weinberg taught in his class on the 48 Ways (with some added explanations).

I have a question: why is this topic a separate one of the 48 Ways? It would seem to be a part of 48 Way #10 – "Seeking Wisdom from the Wise." To get the most out of the wisdom of wise men, you need to give them the benefit of the doubt on issues that you don't have clarity on. And if that idea is enough to make it a separate Way, why not place it right after "Seeking Wisdom from the Wise"? Why is it placed at Way #24, in between Way #23 – "Being a Good Person: Having a Good Heart," and Way #25 – "Enduring and Accepting

Pain"? The Sages were wise men, and there must be meaning behind the order in which they teach.

A possible explanation that comes to me is that a good heart – harnessing your drive to be good – and learning to accept pain are both necessary tools to get from a level of being just good to being great. We explained how a good heart does that at the end of Way #23, and will explain how it applies to Way #25.

Emunat Chachamim, "Believing in Wise Men," is also a tool to go from good to great. In order to become great, a person needs to find great wise people to serve as role models to aspire to. People who have realized great achievements will have a deeper perspective on what is needed to accomplish such goals, and the person who trusts them and learns from them can take advantage of their wisdom. To do this, he or she needs to start with belief in their wisdom and greatness – based on previous evidence, of course.

A Torah example of this is found with the prophet Elisha. The great prophet Eliyahu is told by G-d to find a successor. The Tanach says: "So he went from there and he came upon Elisha son of Shaphat while he was plowing.... So Eliyahu went over to him and cast his mantle upon him. He left the oxen and ran after Eliyahu, and said, 'Please let me kiss my father and mother and then I shall go after you....' He then arose and went after Eliyahu and ministered unto him."

Elisha presumably was already one of the "students of the prophets" who were taught by Eliyahu. But he wasn't Eliyahu's special disciple until then. When he saw the opportunity to serve Eliyahu and learn from him, he jumped at it, trusting in the greatness of Eliyahu, leaving work, home, and family.

Through being with a great man, he became great. When Eliyahu was about to be taken up to heaven alive, Elisha asked from him: "May twice as much of your spirit be mine." He asked for the ability to do twice as many great miracles as Eliyahu did. He was granted it, and went on to become the great leader of the prophets after Eliyahu. Yet when he was introduced to the King of Judah, he was introduced as "Elisha son of Shaphat ... who poured water over the hands of Eliyahu." His greatness came from serving and learning from Eliyahu.

Rabbi Noach Weinberg gave a modern-day example of this, also involving the story of Elisha and Eliyahu. In the Eastern Europe of

the early twentieth century, a woman named Sarah Schenirer realized that the religious Jewish women of her time were not getting
proper education in Torah values from their families, and were being
caught up in the "enlightened" non-religious society around them.
Against great opposition (in Eastern Europe at that time, religious
schooling for women was revolutionary), she started teaching young
women Torah, and training them to be teachers. She developed the
Beit Yaakov movement, which has educated generations of religious
women. According to many today, her efforts made more of a profound impact on the present-day Orthodox world than any other
movement of the 20th century.

In the early years of the Beit Yaakov movement, Rav Noach's
father, a businessman in New York, sent Rav Noach's teenage older
sister from America to Eastern Europe to learn from Sarah Schenirer
how to set up Beit Yaakov in America. He sent her a letter saying:
"Make my daughter twice the person you are!" He explained in the
letter that, if she would think it is a chutzpah to ask that, remember that that is what Elisha asked Eliyahu. And (he continued) if
you would say that Elisha asked Eliyahu for that extra level because
Eliyahu only had to deal with the evil King Ahab, who was a Jew,
and Elisha would have to deal with Ahab's son, whose mother was
Jezebel, an evil non-Jewess – you (Rav Noach's father continued)
only have to deal with the Jews in Eastern Europe. My daughter will
have to deal with the Jews in America!

Rav Noach's sister learned with Sarah Schenirer, and came back
to help start the Beit Yaakov movement in America. She (and her
father) trusted in a great person with a revolutionary idea, and accomplished great things because of it.

Today it isn't easy to find great people you can believe in. But
keep looking out for them, and take the opportunity to serve them
if it comes around. And learn from the great leaders of the Jewish
people, from Abraham, from Moshe, from King David, from the
rabbis in the Talmud. Either way, being around great people or just
studying about great people will help to make you greater.

Way · 25

Enduring and Accepting Pain

❡ G-d created us to use our free will to get pleasure. Pain forces us to use our free will. Because of this, pain is the price we pay for pleasure. The more the pleasure, the more pain there is in achieving it.

❡ To be more focused on avoiding pain than maximizing pleasure is the definition of decadence.

❡ Growth requires pain, so learn the techniques for dealing with pain so that it doesn't prevent you from working to grow.

❡ Better than that, learn to accept pain, and be willing to seek out greater pain if the result will be greater growth.

❡ G-d's intention is always to help you. Make your pain into a growth experience, a way of connecting in a deeper way with G-d.

Way #25 is "Accepting Pain" – *Kabalat Hayisurin* in Hebrew. Accepting pain is not something that is easy for people who grow up in Western society. Rabbi Noach Weinberg used to ask people in his 48 Ways class, and I have done it many times since, "What is the opposite of pain?" Close to 100% of the time, the answer given is "Pleasure." That pain and pleasure are opposites is imprinted on the consciousness of the Western world.

Of course, if you think about it, it is obvious that this isn't true. You can't have two opposites at the same time. You can't be both short and tall, both high and low. But you can feel pain and pleasure at the same time. Run the marathon, climb a mountain, or even play a soccer game – you feel the pleasure of the activity together with a lot of physical pain.

The opposite of pain is comfort. When you are in pain, you aren't comfortable, when you are comfortable you feel no pain.

So why does everyone get it wrong? Rav Noach used to say it was because Western society was decadent. The definition of decadence is equating pleasure and comfort. In Western society today, decadence means that people no longer want to have children, because children are too much money and effort. Marriage is on its way out, because marriage takes commitment, which is painful.

Young people text each other rather than talk to each other, because relating to people takes effort, and effort is painful. They channel surf rather than focus on learning something, because learning takes concerted mental effort. In each case, people avoid pain, while missing out on pleasurable growth experiences.

The reality is that pleasure and pain go together. And not only that, the greater the pleasure, the greater the pain involved. A soccer game requires taking a lot of pain. The physical pain you put your body through would be unbearable if you were paying attention to how your body is feeling instead of being involved in the game.

But loving your spouse and children, having to deal with all their needs, can be much more painful. There is the physical tiredness of staying up with young children in the middle of the night. There is the financial pressure of supporting a family. When your spouse or kids are unhappy, you feel their unhappiness. When they blame you for something, as they often do, you feel the pain of their criticism. If they are going in what you think is an unproductive direction, you feel the pain of that too.

Being good, fighting for a cause, can be even more painful. A cause takes up time you would rather use for other things. It can lead to physical, emotional and intellectual stress. You have to deal with fear of failure. You can go to jail, even die, for your cause.

Living with G-d can be the most painful of all. Doing mitzvot that your body doesn't want to do, fighting desires of the body for negative temptations, continually working to focus your mind and emotions on the ultimate reality, all take a major effort of will and self-control – that is why so few of us succeed in doing it on a consistent basis.

Physical pleasure, love, being good, fighting creatively for a cause, seeking to connect with the transcendental – these are the Five Levels of Pleasure that Rav Noach Weinberg used to teach, based on the Sefer Chinuch. And all of them come with increasing levels of pain – the more pleasure that can be achieved, the more pain you have to be willing to take to get that pleasure.

G-d created us this way, because this world is about using our free will to connect with G-d. Without pain, it would be easy. If there was no pain involved in doing a mitzvah or refraining from doing something wrong, we would all be doing mitzvot all the time.

There is no requirement to have unnecessary pain. If pain will go away with Tylenol, take it. But to really live you need to be ready to deal with the pain that can't be avoided. You can't grow to the fullest extent without getting married, which is painful, or having kids, which is painful. You can't learn the same amount and depth of Torah if you only learn when it is easy and comfortable.

So how do you deal with pain, so that it doesn't prevent you from taking on the challenges of life?

First, teach yourself to be tough. We have the ability to fight our bodies and not give in to pain. If you were ten minutes away from the top of Mount Everest, you wouldn't quit even if your body was screaming in pain.

Better yet, keep your eye on the goal. If you want to get to the top, you'll make it despite the pain. If you are focused on the pleasure of the soccer game, you won't notice the pain your body is going through.

Remind yourself that pain is passing, and results are lasting. When you go to the dentist, you appreciate that it is worth tolerating a temporary pain for the good you will get from having your teeth fixed. Having and raising young children is tiring and stressful, but the pleasure continues even after the pain gets less.

Learning Torah is also a way to deal with pain. The Rabbis say "When you have a headache, study Torah." Being involved in wisdom gets your mind off the pain.

Recognize that, if you want to grow, you have to bear some pain. And if you hold back, you will experience other pain anyway – the pain of feeling that you let yourself down, the loneliness of a life without spouse or children.

GOOD TO GREAT

To get anywhere in life requires painful effort. To be good, to choose life, to live with your wants and not your "feel likes," requires pain. By dealing with the pain, and not letting it stop you, you are able to do things that help you grow as a person and achieve in life.

But to be great, it is necessary to increase your level of pain resistance. Instead of just "dealing" with pain, a great person has to learn to "accept" pain.

What's the difference between dealing with pain and accepting pain?

Let's use the example of going to gym to work out. Someone who wants to be healthy will force his body to go and train. It is painful, but he will deal with the pain because he wants the result.

But someone who wants to be a great athlete won't just take the pain of working out. He will push himself to do harder and harder workouts, taking more and more pain. He knows that the more pain he accepts, the greater will be the results.

In the same way, the person who wants spiritual greatness doesn't just look for the easiest way of doing good. He pushes himself to harder and harder challenges, to doing things that are against his nature. My teacher, Rabbi Noach Weinberg, built Aish Hatorah into an international outreach organization by spending six months a year travelling, away from his family, raising money to keep his institution going. He dedicated his life to public-speaking, teaching, fund-raising and working with all different types of people in order to build his movement, despite being an introvert. He accepted a level of pain that was much greater than most people, and his level of accomplishment was much greater as well.

Accept the pain that is necessary for growth. It takes painful discipline to fight sleep, get up early to pray, talk to a stranger, change your diet to eat healthier foods. It takes pain to break habits, to stop smoking, to accept criticism, to accept responsibility for helping other people, to give charity or to give time to your cause. Keep reminding yourself that G-d rewards you for the pain you take for a good purpose. In Pirke Avos, it says, "According to the pain is the reward."

Accepting pain includes accepting the pain that comes from acts of G-d. When a close relative dies, we don't just deal with the pain we can't avoid by sitting *shiva* and tearing our clothes. We say *Baruch Dayan Emes*, "Blessed be the True Judge." We work to understand and accept G-d's judgment, even when it is extremely painful. When something bad happens to us that we don't understand, we say *Gam zu l'tova*, "this also is for good," and try to understand what that good is.

Remember that G-d's intention is always to help you, "like a father chastises a son." Make your pain into a growth experience, a way of connecting in a deeper way to G-d.

To achieve greatness requires pain. If it was easy to be great, we would all be great. So when you set yourself a high goal, accept in advance all the pain that is necessary to get there. That was what Rabbi Akiva (mentioned at the end of Way #23 – "Being a Good Person: Having a Good Heart") did. He accepted an excruciatingly painful death, happy because he now had the opportunity to give his life for G-d.

Jews don't look for martyrdom. G-d knows what we can handle, and gives us the pain that will help us get to the highest level that we can reach. May we all experience the pleasures of life and growth, with the least amount of pain necessary to achieve our goals.

Way · 26

Knowing your Place in the World

❧ To know your place means first of all to know that you have a unique place in the world. You are responsible for your decisions.

❧ Whenever you hear or learn an idea, ask yourself: do I understand it? Do I agree with it? Do I have enough information to agree or disagree?

❧ Knowing your place also means accurately assessing your wisdom, talents, strengths and weaknesses and comparing them to others. If you know your place compared to others, you know whether to listen or to teach, to lead or be led.

❧ The responsibility of your place is to lead when you are the best person to lead, to work with others who are on the same level, and to follow the person who knows more than you.

❧ A person who does not know his place can cause great damage, whether to his sports team, to his business or to his country.

Way #26 is called *Makir et Mekomo*, which translates literally as "Recognizing One's Place."

When a Jewish court of 23 judges was holding a capital trial, all the judges would sit in a semi-circle seated "according to their level of wisdom." In front of them, three rows each of 23 lesser wise men would face them in case any judges had to be added. They were also seated "according to their level of wisdom."

Imagine trying to do that today, to seat 92 people according to their wisdom! Think of the fights that would break out! Who has an accurate enough assessment of himself to be able to accept that all those people are greater in wisdom than he is? What would all the people who are sitting below him think?

For a Jewish court to operate successfully, it is necessary for a judge to know what his "place" is. But it is also a need for every human being. To be able to properly use your talents and wisdom in life, you need to know how to compare yourself to others.

The first thing to know is that you stand in a unique "place" that no one else in the world stands in. G-d created you to take responsibility for yourself, and you can depend on no one else to take that responsibility.

The Rabbis said that G-d created all human beings from one man, Adam, to teach us that every person should say "This world was created for me." An all-powerful G-d does not have to create a world with seven billion people in it just to use resources efficiently. He could have created a universe for each individual. The other 6,999,999,999 people in your world are there because they help you in some way. You are in their world because you help them in some way.

If the world is created for you, you need to be the one to make the judgments about how to make use of it. In Pirke Avos, Hillel says: "If I am not for myself, who will be for me?" I need to decide what I am going to do. I can't expect anyone else to decide for me, and I shouldn't look to them to decide. G-d will judge me on my decisions, and I can't escape my responsibility by saying the decision was made for me by someone else.

Therefore, whenever you hear or learn an idea, you need to ask yourself: do I understand it? Do I agree with it? Do I have enough information to agree or disagree?

When a much wiser person tells you something, you still have to make a judgment whether to listen to him. In Way #24 – "Belief in Wise People," we said that you should trust a wise man's judgment when he has demonstrated to you his wisdom, or had it attested to by reliable sources. That doesn't mean you have no responsibility. You still have to judge for yourself that you lack the knowledge to decide the issue for yourself. And even if you lack enough knowledge to judge the issue yourself, you still have to judge that the person you are listening to is wiser than you, either from personal experience or because the sources that testify to his wisdom are reliable.

When a great and charismatic leader, who everyone else looks up to, asks you to follow him, you still have to make your own judgment about his cause, what he is asking you to do, how much you trust him and how much you can trust the people who look to him.

After accepting that you need to make your own decisions, you can go on to the next step. You can decide how to relate to others. Knowing your place with regard to others means making a judgment: do I know more or less than someone else? Am I more talented in a certain area, or less talented? Do I have more clarity about what the right thing to do is, or less?

We do this naturally in certain situations. We defer to a doctor over medical issues, because we recognize his greater expertise. We make decisions for our young children because we recognize their lack of knowledge, self-control, and experience.

But in many other situations we don't do that. And when we don't, it causes a lot of problems. Many of us have had the experience of being on a sports team with someone who has an exaggerated idea of his abilities. When he should pass to someone else, he tries to score the winning goal himself, and causes his team to lose. Or we have been at a business meeting where someone who doesn't really appreciate the problem argues at great length for his own solutions and doesn't listen to people who know more than he does.

So before you interact with others, judge yourself. Do you know more or less than this person, are you better at this or is he better than you?

In order to do this, you have to be honest in judging yourself. Know your virtues and faults, know your talents and weaknesses, know what you know clearly and what you are unclear about.

This evaluation isn't always easy to make. Our ego can lead us to exaggerate our own importance or our level of knowledge on a particular subject. Envy of others can lead us to put down other people and downgrade their contributions. Desire for money or status can lead us to underestimate other people's abilities. The Rabbis say in Pirke Avos, "Envy, desire, and the drive for honor take a man out of the world." They confuse us about our place and prevent us from dealing with the reality of the world.

Not knowing your place doesn't always mean having an exaggeratedly high idea of who you are or what you know. It can also mean having too negative an idea of who you are and what your talents are. The Rabbis say: "Don't be a wicked person in your own eyes." Don't let your faults in some areas blind you to the things you do know clearly and can contribute to others.

GOOD TO GREAT

Although recognizing your place applies at any level of growth, it is especially important for the person who is seeking greatness. A truly great person has the responsibility to help others achieve their potential in life.

To do this requires knowing your place so that you can take on the responsibility of your place. If you know more than someone, you have a responsibility to teach and lead. If you know less than someone, you have a responsibility to listen and follow. If you are on the same level, you have a responsibility to share what you know and work together.

We see this quality with Moshe, our greatest leader. Raised in Pharaoh's palace, he steps outside the palace to identify with his people, slaves in Egypt. He sees an Egyptian beating a Jewish slave. The Torah tells us that "he looked this way and that, and saw that there was no man." Having seen that there was no man, he strikes down the Egyptian.

Why does the Torah tell us that he looked both ways and saw there was no man? Does it need to tell us that Moshe was a practical person? Rabbi Noach Weinberg interpreted it as teaching something deeper and more important. Moshe was looking to see if there was anyone else who would do anything about what was happening. When he saw there was no man, he took the responsibility of his place to do something about it. If there had been someone else who could do the job, he would have let that person do it.

In contrast, a person with great leadership abilities who doesn't know his place can become a great tyrant and do great evil.

Yeravam ben Nevat was a man of great talent. He stood up to the popular and powerful King Solomon over an issue where Solomon was making a mistake. He put his life in danger by doing it. The prophet Ahijah the Shilonite met him, as he was running away from Jerusalem, and promised him in the name of the Almighty that he would become King of ten of the Tribes of the Jewish people. When Solomon died, those Ten Tribes turned to him for leadership.

When Yeravam became king of the Ten Tribes, he worried that his subjects would turn against him and return their allegiance to the House of David, which continued to rule in Jerusalem. He took steps to separate the Ten Tribes from the Temple in Jerusalem and from the House of David.

Because he started out as a good man, G-d tried to get him to do *teshuva*. The Midrash says that G-d came to him in a dream, and said to him: "Let Me and you and the son of Jesse (David's descendant) walk together in the Garden of Eden." Yeravam asked: "Who will go first?" G-d said to him: "The son of Jesse." Yeravam said: "In that case I don't want it."

Not wanting to accept second place, he continued to lead the Ten Tribes away from the Temple and a close relationship with G-d. He became the worst person in Jewish history, responsible for the exile and disappearance of 5/6 of the Jewish people.

Every person has a mission in life, something they can do that no one else can do. Knowing your place is a start to knowing your mission. May we all be able to accurately know ourselves and use that knowledge to impact the world.

The Pathway to Happiness: Being Happy with your Portion

¶ Happiness is an emotion that comes from appreciating what you have.

¶ Since everyone has priceless gifts, everyone can and should be happy if they focus on appreciating those gifts.

¶ Play "the happiness game." Write down the blessings you have and add to them every day for 30 days.

¶ A happy person appreciates that G-d is doing His job, both in what He gives us and what He doesn't. An unhappy person will think that G-d doesn't know how to run His universe.

¶ Great people, who are busy trying to change an imperfect world, still need to work on being happy. Knowing that whatever we have is best for us gives us the energy and trust in G-d to go further.

If you ask people today what their goal in life is, many will answer: to be happy. Usually they are people who have gone through a lot of tough times.

In reality, there is much more to life than being happy – to live meaningfully, to accomplish, to help humanity, to gain wisdom, to be in a relationship with G-d.

But happiness is a foundation feeling. If we don't have it, it is hard to see beyond it to other goals. In order to fully live, you have to be happy – than you can open up to the rest of life.

For many people, having happiness is not easy. That's because of two wrong beliefs people have about happiness.

The first is that happiness, since it's an emotion, is a happening. You either feel it or you don't, there isn't anything you can do about it. Either there is a lot in your life making you happy, or there isn't.

The second belief is that, if I had the right circumstances, I would be happy. Yet we see this isn't true. People who have very little can still be happy people, and very rich people with everything going for them can still be miserable, even commit suicide.

Get rid of these wrong beliefs. As mentioned earlier in the 48 Ways, emotions can be worked on by knowing what causes a particular emotion. Happiness can be worked on by knowing the simple definition of what causes a person to be happy. And what causes a person to be happy is available to every person at every time.

Way #27 is called *Sameach B'Chelko* in Hebrew. It means "Being happy with one's portion." The Sages are referring here to the emotion of happiness. By describing it as "being happy with one's portion," we are being told the definition of happiness.

Happiness is a pleasurable emotion that comes from appreciating what you have. If you appreciate that life is good and that you have a lot of good things, you will feel happiness.

The Sages said in Pirke Avos: "Who is rich? The person who is happy with his portion." Bill Gates isn't the richest man in the world. The richest man in the world might be someone we don't know about who really appreciates what he has. It might be you.

How can you see this? Maybe, in contrast to Bill Gates, you just don't have much good in your life! It doesn't take much thought to realize that it isn't true. What amount of money would you be willing to accept for even one of your eyes? Certainly even Bill Gates would give up his billions to not go blind. What about your hands, your ability to walk? And these gifts are nothing in value compared to your parents or your children.

It is true, we all have problems too. But if you lost the use of your eyes for a time, and thought you would become blind, and then got your sight back, wouldn't it make you forget the problem with your boss or the argument with your wife, at least for a few days?

Everyone has priceless things in their lives that have more value than anything material they can expect to get in the future.

So why are we sometimes unhappy, even though we have such priceless things?

The answer is that our feelings are not based on what we have, they are based on what we appreciate about what we have. Human beings have a tendency to take what they already have for granted, and focus instead on what they don't have. With that state of mind, you can be rich and famous and still be unhappy, because there is always something that you don't have.

To train ourselves to focus on what we have and not take these things for granted, Rav Noach taught what he called "the happiness game." Make a list of the spiritual and physical blessings you have that come to mind – your parents, your children, your spouse, your friends, your community, your teachers, your health, your eyes, hands, feet, ears. Anyone can take a half hour writing down what comes to mind easily. Then put a price tag on them. Then prioritize them – hands or feet, mother or father, eyes or parents. Add to the list for thirty days, one every morning and one at night.

By the end of it, it will be blindingly clear just how many valuable things you have to take pleasure in.

In the morning blessings we say every day, the Rabbis set down some of these. We bless having the ability to think, on being Jewish, on being able to see, to stand up, and much more.

You can use those blessings as a start to creating your own list.

GOOD TO GREAT

Being happy is a requirement for achieving greatness and deepening our relationship to G-d. An unhappy person is missing the point of the world. G-d created us in order to give to us. If you aren't happy, you are going to think that G-d doesn't know how to do His job.

A happy person understands that G-d is doing His job, both with what He gives us and what He doesn't give us. Basic Jewish awareness is that we are living in the best of all possible worlds. Since G-d loves us, and understands totally who we are and what we need, and He has all the power to help us, then everything that happens to us, even the bad things, are for the good. What we have is really ours, and what we don't have is not good for us. With that awareness, we can be happy under any circumstances.

Does that mean that we should become complacent and feel no need to change the world? No – G-d created us to change the world, to make it a better place. But, at whatever point we are in that process, being happy with what we have is our foundation. By appreciating what we already have, we know the Almighty will be with us in what we have not yet done.

Way · 28

Being a Realist:
Making a Fence for your Life Goals

❧ A fence is set up to prevent a field from being trampled on. The Sages tell us to set up "fences" to protect Torah laws from being negligently ignored or violated. In the same way, set up fences in your personal life to protect important things that you want to accomplish.

❧ To make a fence for life issues, decide what you want to do, envision in advance the problems that will come up, and work out in advance a way to get around them.

❧ A crucial fence is to set up a regular time for thinking about your life, to counter the desire of the body to go ahead without thinking.

❧ In order to be great, choose the greatness you want to achieve. Then realistically assess the problems that will come up, and work out a plan in advance to counter those problems.

❧ Be a realist, not a hero. If something will make a goal more achievable, use it, even if it seems restrictive or mundane.

In Pirke Avos, the members of the Great Assembly say: "Make a fence for Torah." The Sages instituted many "fences" in Jewish law that protect the laws of the Torah like a fence protects a field from being trampled on by outsiders.

"Fences" in Jewish law are prohibitions based on the Sages'

knowledge of human nature. For instance: on the Sabbath, don't even pick up a pen (which the Torah would allow) because you might unthinkingly come to write with it (which is a violation of the Sabbath).

The need for fences is not only true with regards to law, but is true with regards to the rest of our lives as well. We all want to grow as people and accomplish our goals. Ideally, we should be able to do that simply by making a choice to go after what we believe in. That would be the quickest way. But to be successful in living you need to be a hard-headed realist. Understand your limitations, and plan your way to get around them. That is the meaning of the Hebrew term for Way #28 – *Oseh S'yag l'dvarav*; literally, "He Makes a Fence for His Things."

Where can we see how this works? On Yom Kippur, we are living on a higher level. By the end of Yom Kippur, our idealistic self has come up with some conclusions about how we are going to change, how next year will be different.

But what happens immediately after Yom Kippur? We are no longer on that level of inspiration, so we forget. If we do remember what we decided, we put off doing anything about it. By next Yom Kippur, we are back in the same place.

That has a long-range negative impact on us. Besides the fact that we don't grow the way we could, we lose confidence in our ability to change. The next Yom Kippur, we say to ourselves that it is better not to decide on any changes, because we won't follow through on them anyway.

But that isn't the way we should respond. A realist would say: I could have predicted in advance what would happen. Let me make a fence so that it won't happen again.

In the Yom Kippur example, a fence would be to write down in a book immediately after Yom Kippur what you decided so you don't forget. And if you might put away the book and never look at it, set up in your diary a set time once a month that you look at the book again. And if you ignore even that, organize with a friend to remind you. Or put it on your email calendar to constantly remind you.

This principle of making a fence goes for all the many things in life you would like to do but somehow never do.

Would you like to go on a diet? It is obviously not going to work if you keep too much food in the refrigerator, so get rid in advance of anything except essentials. Since you know that the good meals of Shabbat will threaten your diet, make a plan in advance of what you will and won't eat.

Do you want to spend within your budget? Make a decision to pay in cash, instead of with a card. You won't be able to spend more than your limit.

Relationships are one area where realism requires fences. In the religious world, dating couples make fences against any physical intimacy, even touching, so that premature emotional involvement won't prevent the serious discussions of life-goals that should take place before deciding to get married. In contrast, one couple I know did not make that fence. They didn't find out until they were married that one of the partners badly wanted children and the other one didn't want to have them!

Married couples can get out of touch with each other, and need rules to keep that from happening. A fence would be to check in everyday with your spouse to see how he or she is doing.

This Way is not the same as Way #22 – "Conquering Anger and Frustration." That Way tells you to not give up on things you start to do because they get too hard. "Make a fence for your things" would tell you to plan in advance ways to keep it from getting too hard. An example: if it is your goal to learn Hebrew, don't quit because it is more difficult than you expected and is taking longer. But even better would be to realize in advance that that could happen, and make a fence to make a regular time to meet with a friend who is also studying Hebrew, so you can motivate each other.

Our biggest mistake, according to Rabbi Moshe Chaim Luzzatto in "Path of the Just," is not to think about what we are living for. We always find things to distract us. A fence to avoid that mistake is to take five minutes a day to ask yourself the question. Or even once a week at a set time. Or make an arrangement with a friend to work on it together.

FENCES FOR GREATNESS

I have often asked classes of young people: "Do you want to be great?" Everyone will say yes. We all want to do something special with our lives.

Then I would ask them a follow-up question. If your parents were sitting here instead of you, how many would answer the same as you? Most members of a group of fifty and sixty year-olds would no longer say they wanted to be great, because they realize they haven't achieved greatness. More likely, they would say that they have become more realistic, and have satisfied themselves with raising a good family, being responsible parents, helping their community.

This "realism" is actually a sad commentary on the fact that most of us haven't put the effort into realizing the higher goals we might have had when we were younger.

A better "realism" would be to realistically analyze, when we are still young, what might stand between us and our goals, and make fences to allow us to achieve them.

The first fence, the one people usually don't set for themselves, is to take the time to think: what greatness are you looking for? If you become a great musician, would that be enough to justify to yourself your desire to be great? What if you were a highly successful businessman? What if you succeeded in being head of a major organization that is fighting world poverty? What if you became a top doctor doing work to cure cancer or Alzheimer's? You need to have a goal in order to push yourself to the effort needed to be great, and not to be distracted by everything else that comes up along the way.

Jewish wisdom advises that there are three classes of real greatness: "the Crown of Torah," "the Crown of Kingship," and "the Crown of Kohanim [Priests]." In the world today, that would be being a great Torah scholar and using that wisdom to impact the Jewish world (the Crown of Torah); making the effort to fix up the world, and get people working together to solve the world's spiritual and physical problems (that is the Crown of Kingship, because that was the job of a Jewish King); living your life in such a way that you are a role model to others in how to live spiritually (that is the Crown of the Kohanim, because the job of the Kohen was to demonstrate through action how a person should serve G-d).

If you are committed to any of the three, it takes realism to achieve them. Many of the 48 Ways give tools for how.

If your goal is the Crown of Torah, a lot of problems may arise. We get distracted by the rest of life, and don't put in enough learning time. We learn and forget what we learn. We don't make the effort to deepen our understanding of what we learn. We get distracted by the pressures of supporting and raising a family.

Fences for these include: don't waste any of your time, schedule learning into your evenings and your leisure time; make sure to review what you learn, and work on memory skills – all this is from Way #1 – *Life-Long Study*. Look for opportunities to teach what you have learned, so you will know it on a deeper level – this is Way #12 – "Growth through Teaching: The Questioning of Students." Make a regular time to think more deeply into what you learn – Way #13, "Searching your Mind for Wisdom with Deliberateness." When you are finding it difficult to learn, and you are tired, learn easier things that you are more motivated to learn instead of just reading a secular book or surfing the internet – that is Way #43, which in Hebrew is *Mityashev Libo B'talmudo*, or "Sets his heart in his Studies." And make sure that your goal is part of your decision in choosing who you marry – a spouse who doesn't agree with your goal can make achieving it very difficult. And choose how you will make a living and support your family – what way of supporting yourself will give you the most time to learn?

If your goal is the Crown of Kingship (Rabbi Weinberg, my teacher, felt that, with the crisis in the Jewish world today, this was what Jews should be focusing on), it also takes realism.

First, look for an organization that you think is doing what needs to be done, and join it. In Pirke Avos, it says "be a tail to lions rather than the head of a group of foxes." Dick Horowitz, a California businessman, tells how, wanting to contribute to the Jewish people, he did a systematic study of all Jewish organizations, including personal visits, before choosing Aish Hatorah (where he was able to do many great things in advancing Aish's cause of fighting assimilation). Very few people make that effort, leaving their opportunities for greatness to what comes up by chance.

Second, if you don't see anyone doing what you think needs to be done, work on how to enlist other people in your cause. One person can't accomplish what a group of people working together can. Learn to fund-raise, so you will have the freedom to do what you see is needed, instead of having to do what other people will pay you for.

These are just some of the things that someone who really wants to accomplish his or her goal might think of. To take realistic steps, to plan ahead, to look how to overcome obstacles that may come up, is doing what the Almighty wants. G-d wants successful realists, not heroes. The Rabbis say: "Who is the wise man? The one who sees what will happen in the future." Set your goals, see the problems in attaining them, and avoid the problems. You may get there more slowly, but you will get there.

Way · 29

Taking Pleasure, Not Credit

❡ Taking credit, thinking you are a great and special person, is a deep misunderstanding of the relationship between a human being and G-d.

❡ All your accomplishments are only possible because of the tools given you by G-d.

❡ The fact that you used your free will and made hard efforts to develop the potential of those tools only means that you were smart enough to act for your own benefit. It gives you no moral superiority.

❡ Take pleasure in your accomplishments instead of taking credit for them.

❡ A person, even a great person, who takes credit for his or her accomplishments is likely to have those accomplishments taken away.

The Hebrew term for Way #29 is *Eino Mahazik Tovah L'atzmo,* which literally translates as, "He doesn't consider himself special." It means that we need to learn not to take credit for what we have. We need to recognize that our talents and our accomplishments are all a gift from a loving G-d. They don't make us special, superior people.

This is not as easy as it sounds. Human nature is to take credit for whatever we have that is good and special about us. And since every human being has something good and special about him or her, there is always something to take credit for. There are many words in English for different aspects of this: pride, arrogance, haughtiness, self-aggrandizement, conceit, boastfulness, egotism, self-centeredness, high-handedness. But even people who don't show any of these qualities in an obvious way are likely to be taking credit for something. If nothing else, they can take credit for their humility!

The source for the phrase "considering oneself special" is a Mishna in Pirke Avos. Rabban Yochanan ben Zakkai said: "If you have learned a lot of Torah, don't consider yourself special, because you were created for that."

But why isn't it a good reason to take credit if you are doing what you are created for? How many people are doing what they are created for?

We can understand what Rabbi Yochanan means if we look at people who take credit for lower levels of accomplishment.

A man who is handsome, a girl who is beautiful, will often feel that that makes them special people. We can easily appreciate that it doesn't. Their looks represent no effort on their part, they have just received a gift from G-d.

A sports hero, or an accomplished movie star, will consider that they have more reasons to think they are special. After all, they did have to work hard to develop the talents they have succeeded with.

But this also can easily be shown to be an illusion.

First, what they accomplished could only happen because of what they were born with. A five foot six man will never be a star basketball player, and an unattractive woman will never be a romantic movie star. Their efforts only were successful because they worked with their natural gifts, which were given to them by G-d. Their effort is only developing the potential that G-d supplied them with.

My teacher, Rabbi Noach Weinberg, used to say: If someone gave you a ten thousand dollar check, should you take pride in the fact that you knew enough to take it to the bank, even if not everyone knew to do that?

Secondly, the goal of their effort is only for themselves. They benefit by the effort of taking the check to the bank, and they would lose out if they didn't cash it. Doing what is good for you is smart, but it doesn't make you morally superior to the people who are not doing what is good for them.

But what about a person who doesn't have special talents but used his or her free will and made tremendous effort and self-sacrifice to achieve success? What about a self-made man who fought against all odds to build up his business, a handicapped sportsman who won in the Special Olympics, a plain woman who made herself into a great character actress?

Even in these cases, the factors we mentioned above apply. They are still using whatever abilities they have as human beings, which are a gift from G-d. They are only developing, with their great effort, the potential that G-d gave them. Some checks take more effort to deposit than others. And they are only doing what is good for themselves.

But what if a person used his or her free will and made tremendous effort and self-sacrifice to help humanity, to make themselves righteous and holy people, to become great Torah scholars and teachers?

Rabban Yochanan ben Zakkai tells us that, even in the above cases, don't consider yourself worthy of special consideration, because "that is what you were created for." All the factors we have mentioned previously apply.

G-d created you with the ability to think, to learn, to choose, and to do. Even if you were born without obvious talents, a human being has it all in potential. Your efforts to learn, to grow, to help others, are just using the potential that you were given. You are taking the check to the bank. The fact that the vast majority of people in the world are not banking their checks is because of their deep confusion, not because they were lacking your unique good qualities.

And finally, whatever you do to do more good, to learn more Torah, is benefitting you directly. G-d doesn't need you to learn, He doesn't need you to help other people. Others may benefit from what you do, but you are still acting in your own interest. "Man was only created to take pleasure in G-d," says the Talmud, and your good actions and learning are getting you more of that pleasure in this world and the World-to-Come.

So if you can't take credit, what can you do? Take pleasure in what you have and what you accomplished, like you take pleasure in a gift you have received. We are here to take pleasure, not pride, in what we achieve.

Our natural tendency is to pray to G-d when things are difficult, and congratulate ourselves when we succeed. To counteract this, Eliezer, Abraham's servant, bowed to HaShem whenever he heard good news. When something good happens to you, don't take credit for it, thank G-d instead.

When you grow in wisdom, don't take credit for what you understand. Give credit to the people who taught it to you, and to G-d, who is the source of all inspiration.

If you want to be great and accomplish great things, you have to counteract the human tendency to say, as the Torah quotes, "The power and strength of my hand did this for me." People who think their accomplishments depend on their own efforts will be limited in what they can accomplish, because what can one human being do? But if you know that G-d gave you the ability to accomplish what you have already accomplished, you know that He can give you much more.

The person who has achieved greatness, who is a great Torah scholar or who is making a tremendous difference in the world, needs to be especially careful. It is easy for him or her to take credit for his or her achievement. But when you take credit, you lose your greatness. Greatness is just a large check given you by G-d. You can only cash the check with G-d's constant help. When you become arrogant, or think you deserve praise for it, the check is cancelled.

The great Hillel, in Pirke Avos, spoke about rabbis who take credit for their Torah learning. He said: "The one who builds up his name, loses his name." When you become arrogant, people will see that your wisdom is hollow, because G-d is no longer helping you.

And we can learn the same principle from the fate of evil men. The arrogant King of Babylonia, Nebuchadnezzar, was given by G-d a great empire, including the power to destroy G-d's Temple. But when he said: "Is this not the great Babylon, which I have built up into a royal house with my powerful strength for glorification of my splendor!" a voice came from heaven: "To you, King Nebuchadnezzar, we say: the kingdom has departed from you! We are driving you from mankind, and your dwelling will be with the beasts of the field; they will feed you grass like oxen; and seven periods will pass over you, until you recognize that the Supreme One rules over the kingdom of man and He gives it to whomever He wishes."

May we cash all our checks at G-d's bank, which is open everywhere, all the time.

Way · 30

Love Yourself

- Love is an emotion of pleasure that comes from appreciating the virtues in another person and identifying that person with his or her virtues.

- Before you can teach yourself to love someone else, you have to work on loving yourself. The more you are aware of and appreciate your own virtues, the more you can appreciate them in someone else.

- The way to increase your love of yourself is to get to know your virtues, both those that you share with all human beings, and those that are special to you.

- Appreciate that the virtues you have are basic to who you are, while your faults, even though they may be many, are mistakes you make that you would like to change.

- This Way also includes making yourself beloved by people. Give gifts of love, care, help, and wisdom to others so that they will be open to your virtues. It helps you and it helps them.

Every day in Western society someone comes up with an idea that is worse than yesterday's bad idea. Today's idea is to "Marry yourself." People are marrying themselves with a ceremony in front of parents and friends.

At first glance, we might think there is a valid idea here. What better way to show that you like and accept who you are than to marry yourself?

But Judaism understands that this is unnecessary and hopelessly misdirected. You are married to yourself without going through a ceremony. G-d put your body and soul together, and it is going to stay that way until death do you part.

Since your first and most permanent relationship is with yourself, the rabbis say it is crucial to love yourself. Way #30, in Hebrew "*Ahuv*," means "being beloved." The Sages meant "Be beloved," to yourself first of all.

Today, this is a significant problem. Many people think of themselves in a negative way. They look at themselves as not good, not successful, not competent, not smart, not handsome or beautiful. They wish they were someone other than themselves.

This lack of self-love has very negative consequences. The Torah says "Love your neighbor as yourself." Implied in this command is that if you don't love yourself you can't love anyone else. If you can't appreciate what is good about you, you can't appreciate what is good about others.

Furthermore, when you love someone, you are giving them a gift of yourself. If you don't value yourself, you don't think you have what to give.

If you don't love yourself, you can't see any reason why G-d should love you or help you. In Pirke Avos, Rabbi Shimon says, with regards to prayer, "Don't be a wicked person in your own eyes." If you don't value who you are, you won't expect G-d to answer you.

Finally, not loving yourself will make you ineffective. It is painful to think badly of yourself. The pain you feel will cause you to withdraw from dealing with other people, because dealing with them forces you to focus on what you think are your failings, thus increasing your pain.

So how do you go about loving yourself?

The first step is to internalize one of the most important definitions you will ever hear. *What is love?* Our definition: love is an emotion of pleasure that comes from perceiving virtue in another person and identifying the person with his/her virtues.

We can see that this is true if we ask ourselves: What do we love about our wife, husband, father, mother, or child? A mother, who loves her child unconditionally, still can't say: I love him because he is so selfish and doesn't share with other children. She'll say: I love him because he is lively, intelligent, loving. She excuses his faults and hopes he will grow out of them.

In Way #31 – "Love the Transcendental" and Way #32 – "Love People," we will go further with this definition and show why it is so important in learning to love G-d and people. It is a crucial definition for strengthening your marriage.

The first place to use this definition is in order to love yourself. You love yourself by learning to appreciate your virtues.

Start with the incredible virtues you share with other human beings. You are a soul – a spiritual entity connected with G-d. You are Jewish, with a special soul driven for meaning. You want to do the right thing, even if you don't always live up to your ideals.

That is just for a start, but you have many virtues that are unique to you. Kindness, intelligence, sensitivity, honesty, love of life, creativity, idealism. Not everyone has the same virtues, but all of us have many of them. We need to make a list, keep it with us, and add to the list when we become aware of a new virtue.

But what about the fact that you have faults? Shouldn't you pay attention to those too, and dislike yourself if they are too numerous?

The answer is: with the people you are closest to, you recognize that the faults they have are regrettable but not the essence of the person. So it is for you. The faults you have are things you want to get rid of. They don't define who you are.

It isn't a lack of humility to appreciate your virtues. Humbleness means seeing yourself the way you really are in relationship to G-d, and not having an exaggerated idea of yourself and your own importance. Seeing your virtues is seeing your true self, and appreciating why you are valuable to G-d and to others.

Don't make the mistake of associating liking yourself to what other people think of you. Other people's judgments are influenced by their lack of understanding, their own personal faults, and their social conditioning. In the world today, society makes us feel that "success" is how we should measure our self-worth. Even though there are many good people who aren't "successful" in society's eyes, the idolizing of successful people adds greatly to the pain of the majority who haven't succeeded to that extent.

Another aspect of this Way is to work to be beloved by people.

Getting others to love you isn't a wrong thing to do. It will enable you to both accomplish your goals and help others.

But you can't get other people to love you by manipulating them. You need to make it possible for them to see your real virtues, not fake ones. You do this by giving to people through love, friendliness, appreciation, help, concern, good advice.

The most valuable gift you can give someone is wisdom. When you hear a true idea, think who can benefit from it, and make an effort to give it to them. You will love yourself for caring about others, and others will love you for caring about them.

Love the Transcendental

❡ Love of G-d is a transcendental pleasure. It is the greatest of the Five Levels of Pleasure, and the one we were really created for.

❡ Love of G-d is the fundamental desire of the soul. The drive for meaning in all human beings is just another name for our drive to connect to G-d.

❡ Many mitzvot in the Torah help us to love G-d by having us do actions that a lover does for the one he or she loves.

❡ Appreciating everything that G-d has done for you is a major stepping-stone to loving Him.

❡ The wisdom of Kabbala, the ultimate wisdom about the nature of G-d, is the highest way to acquire a love of G-d, although any study of the Torah will also give us greater wisdom about G-d and helps us to love Him.

The Hebrew title for Way #31 is *Oheiv et HaMakom*, "Love the Place." "The Place" is a description the Sages used to describe the transcendental aspect of G-d, an entity transcending the world. He is the Place of the world, we are all part of Him.

How do you love a transcendental G-d? The late Rabbi Yakov Weinberg (the brother of Rabbi Noach Weinberg) once gave an example of a person who loves G-d. He asked us to imagine a baggage-handler at the airport, whose job is to take off bags as they come out onto the conveyor and place them on the ground for people to come and take them away. It is certainly a dull job, but we know that people will do it for money.

Then he asked us to reframe the job. The baggage handler is told to take the bags off the conveyor and then put the same bags back on the conveyor. Then take them off and put them back on. Do that all day.

There is no extra physical effort involved. Yet we can understand that the baggage handler couldn't do that job for long. Even for much more money. Why? Because it is obvious that the job has absolutely no meaning and purpose. A human being needs some sense of meaning and purpose, even if it is such a mundane purpose as taking baggage off a conveyor to help the airport run smoothly.

That baggage-handler, Rabbi Weinberg said, is in love with G-d, even though he doesn't realize it. The drive of human beings for meaning is really the drive of the soul to connect with G-d, the ultimate source of all meaning.

DRIVE FOR MEANING = DRIVE FOR G-D

How do we know that the drive of human beings for meaning is really a drive for G-d? Firstly, because the concept of meaning has no place in the physical world. No animal has meaning in its life, or feels the lack of it. Refraining from harming a gazelle does not provide meaning to a lion, nor does being a vegetarian bring meaningfulness to a gazelle. A human being doesn't find meaning in carrying out the physical acts of life such as eating or sleeping. Meaning only comes from human beings making choices in life (accepting pain to achieve a goal, choosing to care or to help, etc.).

Yet the meaning inherent in those choices is only "real" if they are made in a world created and run by a G-d who is a source of meaning outside the physical world. If human beings, along with the rest of the world, are just the result of chance combinations of physical matter, then any meaning they find in what they do is an artificial construct. We think what we do matters, but it actually doesn't (which is the difficult problem dealt with by the school of philosophy known as existentialism). The human being who is saving the world has no more intrinsic meaning in his life than the man who grows the world's longest fingernails (a famous picture in the Guinness Book of World Records). And the two of them – who are at least trying to achieve a goal – have no more real meaning in what they do than the person who decides that the ultimate meaning is to be a couch potato.

Without G-d, real meaning can't exist, and we should be able to make ourselves content without it, just as animals do. But our intuition (the angel taught it to us) tells us that meaning is real. The joy that we have when we find meaning, and the existential pain we feel if we don't have it, tell us there must be a G-d. Our drive for meaning means that we want G-d to exist, and appreciate His existence. If we love meaning, we love G-d who is the source of the existence of meaning.

THE GREATEST PLEASURE

Since all human beings have a drive for meaning, all human beings have some connection to G-d, even though they may not be aware of it. But to achieve an even greater connection, we need to identify consciously with our drive to love G-d. Loving G-d, having a transcendental connection, is the highest of the Five Levels of Pleasure and the one we are really created to experience. The Rambam describes the ultimate goal in a poetic way: "A person should love G-d with a great, exceeding and fierce love, until his soul is tied to love of G-d and he is thinking of it always like a person who is sick with love, whose mind is not free from the love of that woman and he is thinking of her always. . . . More than this should be the love of G-d in the heart of the ones who love Him, thinking about Him always, as we are commanded to 'Love the Lord your G-d with all your heart and with all your soul'."

INDIRECT, SEMI-DIRECT, AND DIRECT

When Rav Noach Weinberg taught the mitzvah of "Love of G-d," he taught it from the top down. There is a direct, intellectual way to work on love of G-d, a semi-direct way, a way called "the outside awakens the inside" and several indirect ways. Since love of G-d is very hard for us, we are going to teach it in the opposite order. From the easier less direct ways we can start connecting to the higher ways.

The first indirect way is to get in touch with your desire for meaning and realize it is the first step to love of G-d. We want life to have a purpose. We pursue our goals, seek to make a difference to others, strive to make our families happy, do actions to show our care for Israel and the Jewish people. The root of all this, as we said, is a drive for meaning, the soul's drive to connect with G-d. Appreciate the opportunity when you are involved in something meaningful, and see it as a way to feel love of a G-d who makes meaning possible.

The second indirect way is to appreciate that we are all looking for the transcendental experience. When you appreciate the beauty of a snow-capped mountain in the Drakensberg, what are you appreciating? Is dirt and frozen water so beautiful? We are really seeing beyond that to the transcendental beauty of G-d as expressed in His powerful creations. When you step back and appreciate the beauty of your own child, what are you appreciating? Every parent sees something beautiful in their child that others don't see. The appreciation is really for the G-dly soul that is hidden in the body. Your connection to your child is really a link to something transcendent.

It is very hard to connect with the transcendental on a regular basis. The physical body gets in the way, and it takes incredible discipline and focus of your mind to see G-d's presence in the day-to-day happenings of life. That's why we have to get out of our normal lives to go to the Drakensberg or Cape Town to see it. But if we realize that those experiences are transcendental, and see G-d behind them, we can start to see them more in our daily lives as well.

The third indirect way is through the learning of Torah. The intellectual beauty of the words and thoughts of Torah, the depth of the thinking, the practical wisdom and moral clarity we can see in it helps connect us to G-d who gave us the Torah. This is what motivates people learning in *yeshivot*. We all can get a taste of this beauty and wisdom by learning Torah on a regular basis.

"The outside awakening the inside" means to get your body into doing things that can awaken your emotions. It is easier to control your body than to control your emotions. To become someone who loves G-d, act like someone who loves G-d.

The Rambam, in "Mishne Torah" called his sub-book about the daily mitzvot we do, "The Book of Love." These mitzvot include saying the *Shema*, because we are announcing to ourselves and the world that G-d is the only goal of existence, like a lover reminding himself of the importance of his beloved. When we pray, we are talking to G-d and recognizing how much we depend on Him. Wearing *tefillin* is like the wearing of a wedding ring, to remind ourselves of our special relationship to G-d. The *mezuzah* on our doorposts reminds us that G–d is protecting us. Blessings on food are thanking G-d for all the gifts He gives us. When we do these mitzvot, we should focus on their deeper purpose.

The Rambam, in his *Sefer HaMitzvot*, also includes outreach – bringing others to G-d – as a way to show love of G-d. When you have to explain and defend the virtues of G-d to others, you appreciate them much more yourself.

The "semi-direct" way to get love of G-d is through gratitude. Appreciate how much G-d has done for you in your life. Besides creating you and giving you life, He watched over you like a parent watches over a child, was there to help you through difficult times, and gave you your job, your spouse, your children, your community. He gave you a connection to a meaningful life which is an island of sanity in the crazy world we are living in today.

Finally, the direct way. In the previous Way, we gave the Jewish definition of love, "an emotion of pleasure that comes from appreciating the virtues of another person." When applied to G-d, it means appreciating the virtues of G-d. But since G-d is all virtues, whatever you know and understand about G-d will help you to love Him.

Therefore, the Rambam says, the most direct way to get love of G-d is through knowing about Him. Rambam writes: "When a person thinks about G-d's actions and His wondrous creations, and sees from them His wisdom that is incomparable and infinite – immediately he loves, praises and glorifies G-d and develops a burning desire to know the Almighty, like David says 'My soul thirsts for G-d, the living G-d.'"

Because of this, the ultimate way to possess a love of G-d is to study Kabbala, Jewish mysticism, because it is the ultimate wisdom about the nature of G-d. However, all our teachers have told us that we need to go up the ladder to reach the top. Start with understanding what the Torah teaches you about your life, and then work up towards greater and deeper understandings.

May we all merit to be in touch with our deepest drive for connection with the Almighty, from the baggage-handler to the Kabbalist.

Way · 32

Love People

§ Love is a powerful pleasure, worth much more than any physical pleasure.

§ Love is an emotion of pleasure that comes from perceiving virtue in other people and identifying them with their virtues. Using this definition, we can expand the number of people we love, as G-d commands us to do.

§ We don't appreciate this because we are brainwashed by the Greek definition of love, which is really "infatuation."

§ By giving to others, we are more open to appreciating their virtues and loving them.

§ Loving people opens us up to learn from the wisdom that people have.

Way #32 is called *Ohev et HaBriyot*. Literally it means "Love the Creations." The Rabbis used the word "creations" as a synonym for "humankind," to emphasize that all human beings are special because they are creations of G-d.

When Rav Noach Weinberg taught the Five Levels of Pleasure, he would point out that what makes one level of pleasure different from another is that there is no exchange rate. You wouldn't take any amount of one level of pleasure to substitute for the higher level. His example, which everyone immediately connected to, was that there is no amount of physical pleasure (the fifth and lowest level of pleasure) that can ever replace the love (the fourth level of pleasure) we feel for our children, our parents, our brothers and sisters, and, hopefully, our spouses.

So love is an incredibly powerful pleasure, worth more than all the physical pleasures people spend the greater part of their lives pursuing.

Wouldn't you like to get more of that pleasure? Of course you would!

So why don't we put more time into loving more people, and getting that greater pleasure? Shouldn't we seek the pleasure of love more than the pleasure of a vacation in Mauritius?

We can understand the answer if we examine the programming of Western society, that is embedded in our consciousness. Ask anyone in Western society (and I have done this many times): can you be commanded to love someone? Everyone will answer: of course not. We consider love an emotion we either feel for someone or don't. If we don't feel it, there is no way to work on learning to feel it.

That would seem to conflict with G-d's perception, because He commands us to love. We are commanded "Love your neighbor as yourself" as well as to "Love G-d with all your heart, with all your soul, and with all your possessions."

LOVE *CAN BE* DEFINED

So how can we be commanded? As we have mentioned in the past two Ways, love has a powerful definition. *Love is an emotion of pleasure that comes from perceiving the virtues in another person and identifying them with those virtues.* You love your wife/husband because he/she is kind, caring, responsible, not because he/she is anxious, controlling, or lazy. You love your good friends because they are always there for you, because they can give you important insights, because they appreciate life and are fun to be around. Their faults, and everyone has them, don't seem to you to be equal to their virtues, even though those faults may bother you.

This definition has a second part, as important as the first. If love was only about perceiving virtues, you should love the greatest rabbi of the time more than you love your mother. Even though your mother is great, the greatest rabbi probably has more virtues. But to love, you have to identify the person with his or her virtues. The virtues you see in your mother – the kindness, the caring – are virtues you know are basic elements of who she is. You don't really know the greatest rabbi – the virtues you see are only on the surface.

Once we have the definition, we can understand how we can be commanded to love. Work on learning to perceive the virtues of someone else, and work on how we can appreciate that those virtues are essential elements of the person. If you see those virtues in a deep enough way, you will come to love that person.

THE OTHER DEFINITION OF LOVE

So why are we all programmed with the belief that we can't be commanded to love? It is because we have been programmed with another definition of love.

What is that other definition?

As workers in outreach, we already know not to schedule classes on Valentine's Day. Nothing can stand in the way of the heart with the arrow in it. What does the arrow represent? The Greek god Cupid, who shoots an arrow at someone and he/she falls in love. The Greek idea of love has taken over Western society.

Falling in love obviously can't be commanded. You feel it or you don't. When you feel it you are in love, and when you don't you leave that person and move on to someone else.

This isn't real love. It is the false love that we call "infatuation." It is based on a body desire that causes us to identify false virtues – she's an angel, she is so kind, she has no faults. Those false virtues help convince us that it is greater than just a body desire, until the body stops desiring and we fall out of love. Then we realize that the virtues weren't real.

Real love, based on real unchanging virtues, doesn't come suddenly and doesn't leave suddenly. We don't fall out of love with our parents or our children. If we really love our spouse, we don't suddenly fall out of love with him or her. But infatuation, based on the ever-changing desires of the body, comes and goes.

To work on real love, we have to reorient ourselves away from this false programming. Realize that in every romantic novel or pop song, when they say "love" they mean "infatuation." That's why no one makes movies or writes romantic novels about happily married people.

WORKING ON REAL LOVE

So how do we work on real love? Use our definition.

The first place to start is with your wife/husband. You married your spouse because of his or her virtues. Keep looking for them. Sometimes the stresses of marriage and kids make you forget. Remind yourself of what those virtues are, especially mutual love, mutual responsibility for children, but also intelligence, sense of humor, and many other things. A friend of mine told me he keeps a list in his wallet of all the virtues of his wife, so when they have arguments he can go back and remind himself.

The second place is to start with those people around you. Everyone has virtues that you can learn to appreciate. There are wonderful virtues that all people have – they are souls with free will, and a desire for meaning. Then there are the virtues that we share as Jews – we are partners in a binding commitment to G-d. All Jews, the Rabbis say, are driven to search for meaning. Jews are kind and merciful, stubborn and opinionated, takers of responsibility. And each individual has many other virtues. One person is intelligent and perceptive, another is charitable, another loves life and gives over a sense of joy. Learn to be a gourmet of virtues like other people become gourmets of food.

It is important to recognize that the virtues you see in people are really who they are. We see with our children, who have many faults, that the faults aren't the essence of who they are. So it is with everyone. A virtue, even if it is only one, represents a quality of the soul, and represents who the person really is. Faults, even if they are many, are from the body, and are something he or she would really like to get rid of.

You won't love people right away by making lists. To expand your love of people, you have to make it a long-term goal, to practice over and over. When you find it difficult to see people's virtues, try doing things for them, like Abraham, who took in guests, and Aharon, who loved people and brought them to Torah. That investment in them opens you up to seeing their good qualities.

Loving people is really a way of loving G-d. When you see the virtues of people, you are seeing G-d, the source of all virtues, reflected in them. And not only is it a way of loving G-d, but you can use it to love people more. Recognize that what you are loving is the G-dliness in them.

Loving people is also a tool for growing in wisdom. When you love people, when you see their virtues, you are more open to learning from the wisdom that they have. From one person you can learn courage, from another honesty, from a third person discipline. G-d spread different aspects of wisdom to each of His creations, and the one who appreciates the creations is best able to make use of the wisdom each one has.

Way · 33

Love Doing What's Right

❡ As human beings, we know that we are obligated to do the right thing. But it is much harder for us to learn to take pleasure in doing the right thing.

❡ Doing the right thing is a powerful pleasure, level three of the "Five Levels of Pleasure." When we do the right thing, we are acting like G-d, and feel the pleasure of connecting to Him.

❡ We get that pleasure by doing things we are obligated to do: for other people, for ourselves, or for G-d.

❡ We don't always seek out that pleasure because it might be inconvenient, difficult or uncomfortable.

❡ By focusing on the pleasure and not on the pain, we increase our ability to do good deeds.

Way #33 is *Ohev et HaTzadakot* in Hebrew. *Tzadakot* means "right things." The Way is literally translated "Loving Doing the Right Things."

As we have previously mentioned, love comes from appreciating virtues. "Love Doing the Right Things" means to take pleasure in doing the right things, in leading a righteous life filled with fulfilling obligations.

That isn't so easy. You know you have obligations. Ask yourself: how much, on a scale of 1 to 10, do you feel that you need to be doing the right things in your life, the moral obligations that make you a good person? Most likely, you would answer ten or close to 10. Human beings need to know that they are doing the right thing. It hurts us inside if we feel we aren't good people.

Now ask yourself: How much, on a scale of 1 to 10, do you enjoy doing the right things?

For most of us, the first answer is a higher number than the second. We appreciate that we *need* to do the right thing, but we don't always *enjoy* it. We know we need to give charity – it is part of being a good person. But we are more motivated to go on vacation with that money than use it for charity.

When we live like that, it causes problems. The soul wants to do the right thing, but the body holds back. We look for opportunities to escape obligations. If someone else will help my friend move his house, then let him do it. If someone else will step in to give charity to that poor family, let them get the mitzvah. And even when there isn't anyone else to do something that should be done, we find excuses not to do it. Or we do it and feel resentful about it.

In order to truly make use of your desire to be good, you have to learn to love and take pleasure in doing something because it's the right thing.

How do you do that? There are times when you naturally feel the pleasure of doing the right thing. You found someone's wallet, and called him to return it. Or the waiter left the dessert off of your bill, and you told him so he could charge you the proper amount.

What is that pleasure that we feel when we do something right? It's the third of the Five Levels of Pleasure, to be good. By doing good deeds, we are being like G-d. The connection with G-d you get by being like Him is a serious pleasure.

This is a great pleasure that we are willing to sacrifice other things for, including the pleasure of love. Nelson Mandela, the South African leader, gave up a lot of time with his family to spend 26 years in prison for his cause. In his memoirs, he talked about the pain this gave him. Yet he certainly wouldn't have chosen to give up his cause in order to spend more time with his family. Jews living in Israel understand the power of this also. When there is a war, soldiers in reserve units show up to fight even when they have the option to avoid service.

So why does our body resist doing more things to get that pleasure?

Rabbi Noach Weinberg used to illustrate this issue with a story about a Circle Line cruise around Manhattan. When on vacation, you might take the cruise, one of New York's tourist attractions. Someone next to you leans over too far and falls into the murky and polluted East River. You are a good swimmer, and you dive into the polluted, sewage-infested water (it's an old story, the water quality is better now). After struggling with the panicked drowning person who fell in, and taking some mouthfuls of water yourself, you get him into the lifeboat. Your first reaction is: why did G-d do this to me to wreck my vacation? All you want to do is get back and take a shower. But if someone would ask you years later, what was your most memorable vacation, you immediately would think back to that one. You saved a life, and even now you keep in contact with the man and his children.

We see this in real life, not just in stories. People who fought in wars went through very painful experiences. But they love telling you their war stories, because it reminds them of the pleasure they had in fighting for a cause.

The problem we have with doing good is that it is painful. Sometimes that pain is physical, sometimes it is emotional. If we focus on the pain and not the pleasure, we don't want to do it. Once the pain is over, we can feel the pleasure and realize how great it is.

Remember 48 Way #25 – "Enduring and Accepting Pain." Pain is not the opposite of pleasure, pain and pleasure go together. Pain is the price you pay for pleasure. Make up your mind that you will take the pain that comes with the pleasure of doing the right thing. And don't wait until the pain is over to appreciate the pleasure. Notice the pleasure while you are doing it.

So what kind of obligations can you do to increase your pleasure?

Start with clear obligations. In Western society, the only obligations people really appreciate are to help people and not hurt them, so you can certainly start with those. Love and do things for your parents, your spouse, and your children. Help your friends and your community.

There are also obligations to others that we often aren't aware of. Gratitude, having appreciation for those who love us and help us, is an obligation. Acting with integrity, even in situations that might be a financial loss to us. Being honest in our dealings with other people. Showing real care and concern for others, even when we can't alleviate their situation ourselves. Making an effort to be involved with improving our community or making the world a better place.

We also have obligations to ourselves. To learn Torah (so that we can live our lives with wisdom). Not to waste time, (so that we get the most out of our lives). To take care of our health. To support ourselves and not depend on the community, and more.

Finally, we have obligations to G-d. We need to appreciate what He has given us, and be loyal to His cause and His people. Any time we fulfill a Torah commandment – by praying, returning a lost object, putting on *tefillin* or *tzitzit*, and keeping Shabbat – we experience the pleasure of doing what's right.

By learning to focus on the pleasure of performing good deeds, instead of the pain, we increase our ability to do even more good. People who fulfil their obligations because they have to, are still good people. But the pain or discomfort involved, will limit what they do. For a person to be great, he or she has to be willing to accept and fulfil many obligations, which will certainly entail accepting more pain. People who do that because they desire to do it won't be crushed by that pain, and will accomplish a lot more.

Way · 34

Love the Straight Path

¶ The "straight path" refers to actions that are "beyond the letter of the law," things we are not required to do but should do anyway.

¶ King Solomon said that we were created with an inner sense of what those things are, but our desires cause us to rationalize not doing them.

¶ The straight path involves going beyond the obligation to take care of your parents, and includes feeling gratitude, regularly talking to them and visiting with them. It involves not just being contractually honest in business, but trying to ensure that both sides benefit.

¶ Our two strongest rationalizations for not following the straight path: "It's not required," and "I can't – it's too much for me."

¶ Before you do something, check with your intuition: how will I feel if I do this, and what will people I respect think about it?

Way #34 is *Ohev et HaMeisharim*, "Love the Straight Path." It is similar to the previous Way, "Love Doing What's Right," with a subtle yet important difference.

I remember a talk Rabbi Noach Weinberg gave many years ago to the graduates of the first-ever Aish Hatorah Fellowships from Rio de

Janeiro. Speaking to a group whose main concern was getting a job and making money, he gave what today would be an old-fashioned example. Imagine, he said, a man who wakes up at 4 AM every morning, drives all around the city to deliver milk to make sure that no mother with a young child should be unable to feed her baby. We can't even conceive of the greatness of that man! But if he is doing it because that is the job he is getting paid for, he is just the milkman.

His point was to show the difference between the choices someone makes because he gains from it personally, and the person who chooses what is right *only* because it is the right thing to do.

There are two levels of doing what is right. In the previous Way, we talked about people who are fulfilling their contractual obligations, whether to G-d in His Torah, or to their fellow man. We said that we need to learn to "love" doing these obligations, to appreciate the pleasure it gives us to fulfill them. But there are things that aren't necessarily part of a contract that are also necessary to fulfill our potential as human beings. This is the "straight path," a level above righteousness. We need to learn to take pleasure in that too.

In the milkman example, the milkman has a contractual obligation to deliver his milk early in the morning. He should take pleasure in doing his job efficiently and well. He has the right to earn the salary he gets for doing it. But he has no contractual obligation to be emotionally involved in what he is doing and worry about whether the mothers who need it are getting milk for their babies. Yet, as a human being who has a responsibility for other human beings, he should care. And if he cares, he will make the extra effort to deliver the milk up four flights of steps when someone can't come down, or give milk on credit to someone who can't pay for it now.

This perception of the need to "go beyond the letter of the law" is something that is imprinted in the soul. King Solomon expressed it by saying "G-d created us 'straight,' but we make many rationalizations." We have an innate sense of what the right thing to do is, but we use rationalizations to ignore that inner sense, and to limit our responsibility to "the letter of the law."

For example, the letter of the law is that you need to take care of your aging parents, if it is within your financial capabilities. But we all know we should also feel grateful to them, and visit them and talk with them on the phone frequently. Yet there is nothing written in a book to say how often to express gratitude or how often to visit them. So it is easy for us to rationalize – "I'm busy," "they are difficult people," "they are always criticizing me." The straight path means to ignore those rationalizations and act on the basis of what you know inside.

The difficulty of doing this explains one of the complaints I often have to respond to while raising money for Aish from secular Jewish business-people. Many have had experience with religiously dressed, Shabbat observant Jews who are extremely untrustworthy, even though not necessarily contractually dishonest. For obvious reasons, this seems very contradictory to them, and, in fact, is a *chillul HaShem*, a disgrace to G-d's Name. But there is a simple explanation, although it doesn't excuse the dishonesty. The laws of Shabbat are written in a book, and it is clear what the obligations of Shabbat are. The principles of dealing honestly in business are not written in books (beyond obvious prohibitions such as stealing, cheating, or lying). Because they require judgment, they are open to many rationalizations caused by our desires.

To work on this, it is necessary to be in touch with our inner programming, and take pleasure in it. It is the letter of the law not to be mean to people or to embarrass them, but isn't it the straight path to smile at them and go out of your way to be friendly to them? It is the letter of the law not to cheat anyone in business, but isn't it the straight path to do what you can to help your fellow man avoid a financial loss, even if you aren't doing business with him? It is the letter of the law to give a certain percentage of your income to charity, but the straight path would be to figure out what is most needed, and volunteer your time and money without being asked.

Since we escape from the straight path through rationalizations, it is important to be aware of the most common rationalizations we use. One of the most common ones is – "it isn't the law, so it isn't required." A second one would be "I can't" – it is too difficult for me, it interferes with other plans that I have. Yet often "I can't" means "I don't desire to" – if someone would pay me the money for doing it, I would find the time or overcome the difficulty.

In Pirke Avos, Rabbi Yehuda HaNasi gives a general principle for getting in touch with the straight way. He says to get in touch with "whatever is beautiful to you, and beautiful to your fellow man." He is telling us that we have an inner awareness – if we do something right, it will feel beautiful to us, and if we do something wrong we will sense that it is wrong. By thinking about what we should do before we do it, we can check out that inner awareness in advance.

However, Rabbi Yehuda adds that we need to check out what is beautiful to our fellow man. He means: since we are not always in touch with ourselves, and sometimes convince ourselves that the wrong thing is the right thing, we need to do something to help us guard against rationalizing. Ask yourself what your friend, teacher, or someone you trust, would think. By putting the two together, you live your life doing things that are above and beyond what is in the books.

Way · 35

Love Accepting and Giving Criticism

¶ "Love accepting and giving criticism" means to see the virtue and benefit of both receiving criticism yourself and criticizing others for their mistakes.

¶ If people really want to achieve results, they will love and appreciate the criticism that will help them achieve those results through helping them fix their mistakes.

¶ The best way to get good and objective criticism is to ask for it.

¶ If you care about other people, you will love and appreciate the opportunity to help them by pointing out their mistakes.

¶ In today's world, the biggest mistake most people make is not taking advantage of the benefits of Torah and a Torah lifestyle. Love showing people this mistake in a way that they will be able to see it and be willing to listen.

I don't know about you, but I don't like to be criticized. I don't mind criticizing others, but I have found through many years of experience that others don't seem to like receiving my criticism either.

So Way #35 – "Love Accepting and Giving Criticism," (*Ohev et HaTochachot*) would seem to go against human nature. And that goes for both aspects of this Way. It is hard for us to love being criticized, and we can get ourselves in a lot of trouble if we love giving criticism.

PART I: LOVE BEING CRITICIZED

Certainly we have a lot of good reasons not to love being criticized. It's painful – we don't want to think that we have faults. It seems to indicate that people don't like or respect us. It makes us think negatively of ourselves, and none of us like that. It may put pressure on us to change, and change is painful and unsettling.

So how can we learn to love criticism?

First, appreciate there are times when people do welcome criticism.

A politician hires image consultants who tell him that he should look, speak and dress differently.

If someone would come and tell you "You left your headlights on" you would welcome being told. Even if he said "You jerk, you left your headlights on" you probably would thank him.

When people have marital difficulties, they go to a marriage counselor who often will give them heavy criticisms.

Why are people happy to get criticism in these situations? Because we appreciate the consequences of not being criticized. The politician could lose the election, your battery could go dead, and your marriage could get worse.

This is a principle you can apply to any criticism that you receive. Life has important consequences, it isn't limited to politics, cars, or marriage. If you want to succeed at living, you need to be using all your potential. Being made aware of mistakes you are making helps you change, avoid the negative, and achieve the positive.

If you are a teacher, and someone tells you that you speak above people's heads, that's painful. But if you want to be an effective teacher, you need to know so that you can learn to teach effectively.

If your wife tells you that she feels you are insensitive, it's painful and maybe seems unfair. But if you value your relationship with your wife, it is an indication that you need to make changes.

If your spiritual advisor tells you that you are wasting your life and brings evidence, the criticism will hurt, but it can lead to improving your life.

You can limit the pain of criticism, and therefore make it easier to receive, by reminding yourself of a few basic principles.

First, nobody is perfect, we all have faults. Faults don't indicate we are bad people. We are souls, we want to be good and want to get rid of our faults, so even serious faults don't determine who we are. A proof of that is the spiritual uplift we get by doing *teshuva* on Yom Kippur, and the efforts we make on that day to act differently and change ourselves.

Also, remember that pain passes but the results are lasting. If you change for the good because of criticism, you have grown permanently, while the pain you felt from the criticism goes away quickly.

The best advice for receiving criticism is not to wait for people to criticize you. Seek it from them. Most people are afraid to criticize, even when they see things that you are doing that deserve criticism. If you ask them what criticisms they have, they will tell you.

Appreciate that not all criticism is valid. People's perceptions can often be mistaken. But don't jump to answer criticism and justify yourself. Say thank you, and go back and think about it. The Rabbis say "judge everyone to the side of merit," even the one who is criticizing you. Even when you think the criticism is unfair, see if there is some aspect of it that you can learn from.

One of Rav Noach Weinberg's favorite one-liners was, "the battle for life is a battle for sanity." Human beings are fighting a war with themselves, to see things the way they really are and to focus on what's important instead of following after the desires of the body. Look at criticism as a tool for sanity. Someone giving you objective feedback on the things you are doing wrong helps you overcome the insanity of the body, which is always trying to avoid anything that would require you to change.

PART 2: LOVE CRITICIZING OTHERS

This way has a second aspect, to learn to love giving criticism. This is actually one of the 613 *mitzvot*, the mitzvah of *tochacha* – "giving criticism," related to the word "to show" or "to prove." The Torah commands that when you see people doing something wrong, you are obligated to let them know that they are making a mistake.

This 48 Way adds to our understanding of the Torah mitzvah that you need to learn to love doing this. You need to see the virtue in helping others this way, because it will be impossible to succeed at it if you don't appreciate how beneficial it is for the person you are criticizing.

To love giving criticism isn't easy to do. People can react negatively to being criticized. Unless we feel personally hurt by what they are doing, the easiest path seems to be to stay out of it and let them live their own lives and make their own mistakes.

In reality, if someone is in trouble, we can't respect ourselves if we stay uninvolved.

Imagine you are passing the scene of an accident. Someone is lying in the street, and you know basic first aid. Would you be happy with yourself if you didn't help?

During climbing season at Mount Everest, there are always stories of climbers who pass by other climbers dying in the snow because they don't want to lose out on their own summit bid. Would you feel justified to be one of those climbers?

When the physical danger to others is clear, we recognize that we really should do something. But the same principle would apply to someone who is suffering emotionally. What if someone is depressed, and you have the wisdom or caring that could help them? What if someone is wrecking their marriage, and you could give them some sound advice? It is often harder to help someone emotionally than it is to help them physically, but we can appreciate that we have the responsibility to try.

We have this responsibility even if the person doesn't want the help. If we saw a person bleeding on the street, would we stop trying to help him if he said "don't bother me"?

But what if people are leading their lives with no obvious physical or emotional problems? What if their only problem is that they aren't connected to G-d, to Torah, to Judaism? We might think that it isn't our problem, it is G-d's problem – let Him take care of it.

But that isn't the Jewish understanding. We appreciate that there is no worse problem a person could have. To live your life without true meaning is a terrible loss. And the fact that most of the people who suffer from it are unaware of what they are losing only makes it worse.

This is the reason for the Torah mitzvah "to give criticism." When you see a person living their lives in a way that is lacking Torah, you need to try to help them by showing them that Torah is the true meaning to life. This is a fundamental motivation for Jewish outreach and the fight against assimilation, and a major reason why

Rabbi Noach Weinberg set up his organization, Aish Hatorah in Jerusalem, and started teaching the 48 Ways.

Obviously, if the goal is to help them, you can't give criticism by coming down on them. That will only turn people off. The Hebrew word for criticism, *tochacha*, as mentioned, comes from the word *l'hochiach*, "to show" or "to prove." It is necessary to show others that they are losing out by not having Torah and will gain by embracing it.

It takes wisdom to do this. But everyone can start the process by giving over to a secular friend ideas of Torah that they find valuable. Or invite someone for Shabbat. Or connect him or her to your rabbi or rebbetzin.

Don't be put off by thinking: they are happy, why should I get on their case? While it is true that some people are happy even without Torah, mostly because of family and children, they would be even happier with Torah. And for most people today, it isn't like that anymore. The family structure is collapsing, work is not a meaningful substitute, and there is a limit to how long a person can keep his life going through entertainment and social media. Helping people through giving them Torah can be as life-giving as giving oxygen to a dying person on Mount Everest.

Don't give up on people and think that there is no way to reach them. The Midrash says that G-d never took back a positive promise except in one case. Basing itself on lines from the prophet Ezekiel, the Midrash says that G-d had instructed the angel in charge of destroying Jerusalem at the end of the First Temple period to go easy on the people who were completely keeping the Torah. But G-d's attribute of justice said to G-d (metaphorically): what is the difference between the people who are keeping Torah and those who aren't? G-d answered His attribute of justice: these people are totally righteous and the others are wicked! The attribute of justice said: But did those righteous people do anything to reach out to change those wicked people? G-d answered: I know it would not have worked! The attribute of justice said: You knew, but did they know? G-d agreed with the attribute of justice, and told the angel: Start with them.

If G-d is testifying that He knew the wicked people wouldn't change, they must have been a tough and unreceptive group of people. Yet the righteous people, who couldn't know for sure, are blamed for not making the effort. All the more so in our generation, when most Jews seem open to Torah if it is presented in the right way that speaks to them.

G-d places a difficult responsibility on us. But if you love giving criticism, you will never have to be one of those about whom it can be said "he could have made a difference, but he never tried."

Way · 36

Distance Yourself from Honor

❡ Seeking honor from others is a counterfeit of the Third Level of Pleasure, – "being good." When others think we are good, we can convince ourselves that we are good even when we aren't living in a good way.

❡ Since other people's opinions are often mistakes, to seek honor from others confuses us about what is really good.

❡ If you think for yourself, have self-respect, or are involved in a greater cause, you won't care as much about what other people think of you.

❡ Avoid getting honored, if you can. When it is necessary to accept honor, because it helps you to accomplish a greater goal, do something to deflect its impact.

❡ The person who runs away from honor will be able to accomplish more, because he can do what is right without worrying about what others think.

We have mentioned the "Five Levels of Pleasure." The lowest level is physical pleasure – very useful, but not comparable to the greater pleasures. We discussed physical pleasure in Way #18 – "Minimize Physical Pleasure (But Learn from it also)." The second level is "love" which is covered in Way #30 – "Love Yourself" and Way #32 – "Love People." The third level, even higher, is to be good – we dealt with that in Way #23 – "Being a Good Person: Having a

Good Heart," and Way #33 – "Love Doing What's Right" and Way #34 – "Love the Straight Path."

Since life is about the challenge of using free will, G-d created every level of pleasure with a counterfeit pleasure that seems like the real thing. It takes great effort to choose the pleasure over the counterfeit.

The counterfeit of physical pleasure is lust, a body desire that feels sensational in the short run, but doesn't give you the spiritual pleasure that the gourmet will get from food or other real physical pleasures. The counterfeit of love is infatuation, inventing false virtues to make a body desire seem holier than it really is.

Since being good is such a powerful pleasure, it needs to have an equally powerful counterfeit. "Honor," *kavod* in Hebrew, is something that gives you an artificial sense of being a good person. If we don't work on understanding what is wrong about it, and keeping ourselves from it, we are very likely to accept it in place of the real thing. Being able to do this is the focus of Way #36 – "Distance Yourself from Honor."

Every human being has a desire for *kavod*. That is why social pressure is such a powerful force. People need to wear the right style of clothing because they worry what others will think of them. Women spend major amounts of money on how they look. Students spend years getting a university degree, even if they could get a job without it, so that people will see that they have what it takes. Wealthy businessmen seek honor from their peers, pay money to be honored at dinners, and put their names on synagogues or opera houses.

In subtler forms, we even seek honor from people for real virtues that we have. A woman who is a real doer of kindness will skillfully manage the conversation so that it gives her a chance to talk about the kindness she does. An intelligent man will try to get people to recognize his cleverness. A humble person will have to fight the desire to be appreciated because of his or her tremendous humility.

We want it so much because the most powerful need of all human beings is to be good. And it is difficult to know whether you are good or not. Ask an evil man and a good man, "are you a good man?" The evil man is likely to be more convinced of his goodness than the good man. He believes in his rationalizations, while the good man may have self-doubts. Lacking clarity of the standards for being good, we look to other people to supply the standards. If other people think we are good, we can relax – it must be that we are good.

This desire, which we all have, can hurt us in many ways.

First, in order to get honor from people, we have to adjust to their standards. Often these standards are wrong.

Society today judges us on whether we are successful – rich, famous, or accomplished. But successful and good aren't the same. Often the successful man has a bad marriage or trouble with his children yet society gives him a great deal of honor. The person who struggles to make a living, but works on his marriage and taking care of his kids will often be made to feel that he is a loser (and sometimes even his own family will have this reaction).

When we seek society's approval, we push for success even when we know it's not right, and we don't make the effort for things we know are right because others don't approve of them.

In Pirke Avos, Ben Zoma says: Who is the wise man? One who learns from every person. Who is the strong man? Someone who controls his desires. Who is the rich man? The person who appreciates what he has.

Wise, strong, and rich are positive qualities to have. But they are also respected positions in society. Ben Zoma tells us that the real possessor of these qualities may be someone not known to anybody. Your friend may be wiser than Einstein. Your gardener may be stronger than an Olympic medalist. Your neighbor may be richer than Bill Gates.

It makes sense to put your efforts into the real manifestations of these valuable qualities. But then no one will know who you are! If you don't have clarity about what is real in life, the desire for honor will push you to be the sports hero or the rich man, even though it may hurt your life in other ways.

Second, seeking honor gets you into play-acting. You act a certain role because people give you positive feedback. Politicians often lose whatever idealism they had because of the constant need to be honored by others. The same can happen to religious leaders, philanthropists, and social activists.

Finally, when you receive honor it makes you complacent about working on greater personal growth. You feel like you have already arrived, since everyone thinks you have.

So how do you distance yourself from honor? Work on self-respect, appreciating your virtues (Way #30 – "Love Yourself"). If you know the good qualities you have, you don't need other people telling you about them.

Live for a goal (Way #7 – "Living with Humility"). If you have a real cause in your life – helping the Jewish people, becoming a Torah scholar, raising your children to be special individuals, doing acts of kindness – you know you are doing something good, and don't need to be told by others.

Work on thinking for yourself, a quality that can be strengthened by Way #4 – "Connecting with Your Intuition: Understanding of the Heart," and Way #13 – "Searching your Mind for Wisdom with Deliberateness." When you are clear about what you know and what matters in life, you won't feel the pressure to conform to the often wrong ideas of society.

Avoid honors, when you can. Sometimes you need to accept honor to accomplish your goal, but limit it to the minimum. Avoid flattery. Mark Twain used to say, when introduced with great praise before giving a speech: "My daddy would have appreciated it, my mommy would have believed it."

Never stand out and be in the limelight unless it is necessary. In the business book "Good to Great," the author analyzed 15 companies who outperformed everyone in their industry over a long period of time. He found that all these companies had CEOs who avoided the limelight, in contrast to the very public and publicity-seeking CEOs of other companies. By staying away from honor, they were able to concentrate on their true goals and succeed at them. We may have different, and more spiritual goals, but the same principle applies.

Way · 37

Making Everything New: Not Becoming Complacent in your Studies

¶ G-d created a world that is full of meaning and full of opportunities for growth. Don't treat anything in this world as boring or mundane.

¶ Since growth involves effort and change, the body will work to prevent you from exploring these opportunities. "I'm bored," "there's nothing to see here," "I've heard that already," "been there, done that" are excuses of the body.

¶ Always try to look at wisdom or life experiences in a new way, as a child would.

¶ Look at those things you "can't" do in a new way. See that many of them are actually possible.

¶ Be open to the opportunity for growth that may come when you least expect it. The Sages say that you can acquire your World-to-Come in a moment.

The Hebrew term for Way #37 is *Aino Megayes Leebo B'talmudo*, "He doesn't satiate his heart in his studies." It means that you should work on making everything in your life fresh and new, not treating anything in the world as boring or mundane.

I am a *ba'al teshuva* from many years ago, but I still remember my mindset from back then. For a time, I drove a cab in New York City. On the radio, I would be listening to the baseball games, rooting for my New York teams. I distinctly remember thinking to myself: why should I care who wins? And I remember telling myself that if I keep thinking like that, I won't be able to listen to the game anymore, and I will be bored. So I had to make an illogical decision to care who wins a sports game so that life would seem to have meaning.

In reality, that is a lesson about the nature of secular life. If there isn't a G-d, or G-d really has nothing to do with the world, there isn't anything really meaningful that is going on in it. There are exciting experiences every once in a while, but most of life doesn't have much purpose. Shakespeare wrote in Macbeth, "Tomorrow and tomorrow and tomorrow creeps in this petty pace from day to day," and the philosopher Thoreau wrote that "the mass of men lead lives of quiet desperation."

A secular person will not like the meaning of what Shakespeare or Thoreau wrote, but will have a hard time logically arguing against it. Only by filling his or her time with sports, socializing, travel and entertainment can he or she keep ahead of the boredom and mundane nature of a world without G-d. And even though social and political causes, or family can provide somewhat of a substitute, in today's world these are becoming less and less important, while entertainment and social media 24/7 are more and more the norm.

When I realized there was a G-d and that Torah was true, the world became a different place. G-d created a world where everything has a meaning, and opportunities for learning are always available. Every event has a purpose behind it. Every person has tremendous depth – we only use 5% of our minds. And G-d gave us a Torah that teaches us everything we need to know about living. In Pirke Avos, it says "don't despise any person, and don't separate yourself from anything, because there is no person that doesn't have his time, and no thing that doesn't have a place."

In a world like that, there should be no reason ever to be bored. Life should be growth every day.

It doesn't always seem to work that way, because we are souls with bodies. The soul wants growth and wisdom, but the body doesn't want to make an effort. Growth is an effort, and the body fights against it. One of its major techniques is boredom – been there, done that. Nothing new to learn or do. It was exciting at the beginning, but now it's mundane.

This Way, "don't satiate yourself in your study," focuses on the absolutely crucial need to reenergize yourself to the potentials of a world that was created by an infinite eternal G-d who gave us a Torah of infinite depth.

To do that, you first have to recognize how the body works. Just think of the life-changing idea we presented in Way #32 – "Love People." We gave the Jewish definition of love as "an emotion of pleasure that comes from perceiving the virtues in another person and identifying them with their virtues."

Perhaps you thought at the time – that's an exciting idea, to understand a concept that most of the world can't explain! It can give me a tool to increase my pleasure, to help my marriage! I can look at my spouse or my friends, and see if I can see their virtues! Maybe I can teach it over to one of my secular friends as a life-changing idea from Judaism!

You may have thought that at the time, but what if I tell it to you again now? "Been there, done that. Why don't you tell me an idea I don't know?"

You became bored with the idea, yet you haven't necessarily thought deeply about it. How does it change your world view? What potentials might it open up to becoming a more effective person? How can you use it to love your wife more or find new friends? What does it tell you about the society you live in, which spends billions of dollars promoting the idea that love is something you fall into and fall out of?

This thought pattern can also pervade areas other than learning. When you first met your spouse, you were excited. Do you feel that very same excitement today?

So what can you do? Approach life like a child for whom everything is exciting and new. When you hear an idea, don't just say: I've heard it before. Instead, look at it as new, and think about it – what questions do I have, is there a way I can use this, who do I know that would benefit from this idea? When you meet a person, even someone you have known for a long time, ask yourself: what don't I know about them?

Jewish law gives opportunities to remind yourself that life is new all the time. When you wake up, say "*Modeh Ani.*" G-d gave me back my soul for a reason, what should I do with it today?

We say "*Shema*" at least twice a day. It isn't just a mantra, it is giving us a new opportunity to remind ourselves what life is really about.

Periodically, take the time to ask yourself: what am I living for? You may have changed and grown from the last time, and will have a different clarity.

Rav Noach Weinberg gave a particular exercise for this way, to help in looking at things in a new way. Make a list of some things that you "can't" do. You can't spend an extra hour learning per day. You can't afford to have another child. You can't come to *minyan* every morning. You can't get more involved in helping to reach out to Jews.

Examine the list closely. Are they really things you *can't* do? Or you really can, but you don't want to? Or maybe you really want to, but your body doesn't feel like it? Is it something that you might be able to do if you took the time to think out how to do it? Why aren't you taking that time?

To see the possibilities for growth and change, take one "I can't" and make a plan to do it.

Never be bored with life. The Rabbis tell us that there are people who were able to acquire the World-to-Come in one moment. They had a deep realization or were presented with an opportunity for greatness and they took it. At any moment, if you are awake for it, you may have that realization or opportunity. If you are bored with life, you may miss that opportunity when it comes.

Way · 38

The Seriousness of Giving Advice: Not Taking Joy in Teaching Others What To Do

¶ The advice we give has consequences. People can have their lives changed for good by receiving good advice, and their lives can be seriously harmed by accepting bad advice.

¶ Therefore, take the responsibility of providing advice very seriously. Do it only when you are confident that what you are saying is accurate. Don't give advice just to feel important.

¶ Teach yourself to say "I don't know" in a situation where you aren't sure.

¶ If there is someone else who understands the issue better than you, let him or her give the advice.

¶ If you have to give advice when you are not totally sure (because there is no one else available to offer advice about this issue), make sure that you tell the person you are advising what your level of clarity is.

When I was a teacher at Aish Hatorah in Jerusalem, we used to deal with many young Jews who came to Israel to travel. Rabbi Meir Shuster would pick them up at the Kotel, and bring them to Rabbi Noach Weinberg. Rav Noach would persuade them to spend a short time checking out the yeshiva. A significant number of young people, after staying a short time, would decide to stay a longer time. They became observant and now, many years later, are parents of large families and respected members of orthodox communities all over the world.

Today, very few people have the courage of those young people who chose to change their lives so totally. Some of them quit university to study in yeshiva. One of them, who is now a leader at an Aish branch in America, quit medical school. Many of them had serious fights with their parents, who were not happy with their decisions. Many had to put up with friends thinking that they had been brainwashed or gone crazy.

Their decisions were their own decisions. In Aish Hatorah, we didn't brainwash or change people's minds by bombarding their emotions. However, we did try to help people make those decisions, by advising them and letting them know why we thought these were the right decisions. Many of the people we advised took our advice, and went on to lead happy and productive lives.

We had our share of failures as well. People we worked with went home to visit their non-religious families. Needing a place for Shabbat, they would spend Shabbat by people in the local religious community. And sometimes their hosts would give them advice like "go to a real yeshiva!" or "finish college first." Sometimes they would take that advice. Because the advice wasn't based on really knowing the person or understanding the outreach experience, there were sometimes negative consequences that resulted from it.

We made our own mistakes also. Years later, some of the people we advised blamed us for giving them the wrong advice.

I once asked Rabbi Weinberg why heads of yeshivot had to spend so much time travelling to raise money (at certain periods in the history of Aish Hatorah, he was on the road for 6 months of the year). He told me something he had heard from the great Rabbi Aharon Kotler, the head of Lakewood yeshiva: "The head of a yeshiva is responsible for the lives of his students. The law in the Torah is that an accidental murderer gets exiled." If you are constantly advising people, you are going to have consequential mistakes along with your successes.

I came out of my experience at Aish with a strong realization that decisions have heavy consequences for people's lives, and advising them to make those decisions is not something to be done in an unserious way. That is the point of this Way – *Eino Sameach B'hora'ah* – "Don't take joy in teaching others what to do." Take the consequences of others' decisions very seriously, and be very careful in advising others to make them.

That isn't always easy for us. We can see how difficult that can be when someone asks us for directions. If we are in a place that we are unfamiliar with, it is easy to say "I don't know, I'm not from here." But if it is our home neighborhood, and we should know, we feel stupid if we say we don't know. We try to give directions. The result may be that the person we are directing gets lost.

The desire to be in the know and give directions, even when you don't know, is not so hard to deal with when it is pointed out. But what about more important issues? What if someone asks you why you believe in G-d, or why you don't? It isn't so easy to say "I haven't really thought about it."

In Way #2 "Listening" – talking about the need for proper definitions – we told a story from Rabbi Noach Weinberg about dealing with a young man who claimed to be an atheist.

Rav Noach would say: "That's great! I always wanted to meet an atheist! An atheist is someone who knows there is no G-d. So you must have evidence. What evidence do you have?"

Since the young man hadn't thought about it, he didn't have evidence. So he would say: "I meant to say that I am an agnostic." Rav Noach would say: "An agnostic, that is great also! An agnostic is someone who knows that it is impossible to know whether there is a G-d. So you must have evidence of that. What is it?"

Since the young man had no evidence of that either, he would be forced to admit: "Rabbi, I don't know whether there is a G-d." So then Rav Noach would say: "So you don't know, we have evidence!! Come in and I'll teach you."

The relevance of that story to this Way is that a person would rather think he is an atheist, someone with a thought-out philosophy, than admit to being ignorant. As long as he thinks that, he doesn't feel he needs to learn anything. And a sad further consequence is that, when a Rabbi isn't around to counter him, he probably advises others that there is no G-d, tells them to stay away from anyone who is religious, and tells any friend of his who has been to classes on Judaism that he is being brainwashed.

In these and other situations, our mistake is to think that we know what to say, when we actually don't. What about a case in which you do believe that you have clarity? In that case, your responsibility is to teach and do the best you can to help the other person make a correct decision. It is wrong to give advice based on a lack of knowledge, but to refrain from giving advice because you don't want to take the responsibility is also wrong. You are responsible for the consequences if someone takes your wrong advice, and it has a negative impact on their life. But you are just as responsible if someone does something negative for himself because you didn't tell him what you know.

Even when we know something, we still have to judge just how solid our knowledge is. We have some experience in raising our children. Younger parents can benefit from our advice when it comes to choosing what school they should send their children to. But before we give that advice, we need to judge just how sure we are of what we think. Do we fully understand the other person's situation? Is it similar to ours or different?

The answer in many situations like this is not to refrain from advising. People need help from the wisdom and experience of others. But teach yourself, in these cases, to say: this is my opinion, I could be wrong.

A basic principle for deciding when you will advise people – if there is someone else that the person could and would go to who understands the issue better than you, let that other person do the advising. But if there isn't, make sure that the person you are advising is clear what level of knowledge you have, so he or she can accurately judge your advice.

The bottom-line to helping others is to realize that wisdom has real consequences. People lead their lives based on what they understand. If you tell people true ideas that they didn't know before, you may totally change their lives for the good, like the people we convinced to stay in yeshiva so many years ago. Mistaken ideas, given over as if they are thought-out wisdom, can also change a person's life.

The Rabbis say: "Teach your tongue to say 'I don't know.'" Then you won't be in a situation where you can give bad advice that can seriously impact someone else's life.

Way · 39

Caring for People:
Carrying the Burden with your Fellow Man

¶ It takes effort to remove ourselves from the self-centeredness that comes naturally to us, in order to see and care about other people's problems.

¶ We must first learn to be aware of the problems other people have. This is done by recognizing our own problems, understanding problems people have in general, and appreciating problems that are specific to our generation.

¶ When you pay attention to other people's problems, make an effort to show your concern and feel their pain.

¶ Don't hide yourself from the problems of the Jewish people today, or the problems of humanity.

¶ When you feel other people's pain, try to help them. If you can't help them, even showing them that you sympathize with their pain will help them realize they aren't alone.

In the Hebrew text, Way #39 is called *Nosei B'ol im Chavero* – "Carrying the Burden with your Fellow Man" – i.e., caring about them and their problems. It is the first of four Ways that gives a Torah picture of how to deal with and help others. Psychologists should take note – much valuable psychological insight is contained in these four Ways.

Caring about others is not something that comes naturally to us.

One of my colleagues in Jerusalem, Rabbi Motty Berger, gave the following example:

Imagine that one sunny morning you sit down with a pitcher of orange juice to read your morning newspaper. The headline describes a devastating tsunami in Indonesia, and 200,000 people have been killed.

You are a good, decent human being, and you feel bad hearing about such a disaster. But while you are reading about it in the paper, you accidentally knock the pitcher off the table, and it breaks on the floor. The orange juice spills all over.

Which makes you feel worse?

We all know the answer, and we shouldn't feel bad about ourselves. That is the way G-d programmed us. In the Talmud, it says that G-d created all human beings from Adam so that we should all say "the world was created for me." Since we are imprinted with the understanding that "the world was created for me," we all look at the world through self-centered lenses.

But we aren't living in reality if we continue to look at the world that way. We share a world with other human beings, and we need to recognize that they are as real as we are.

To do so, acknowledge that other people are similar to you. Even though we may look different from one another, we all have eyes and ears and a nose. We all have feelings and ambitions, and share a drive for meaning and a drive to be good. And everyone has their own struggles and issues to deal with as well.

To care about other people's problems, you first have to identify what they are.

Sometimes, the problems are so extreme that you can't miss them. On a recent trip with a group to India, I met an intense, intelligent, sensitive young man of 16 who is living in a shelter for homeless street kids in Delhi. When he was 6, his mother took him to a festival and "lost" him in the crowd. He never saw his parents again. A worker at the shelter said that he has a problem trusting anybody, and it isn't hard to understand why.

On the same trip, we went to a café run by women who have been facially disfigured in acid attacks by ex-boyfriends or by vicious mothers-in-law. They run the café to help each other and to bring attention to this serious societal problem.

In comparison, the challenges most of us deal with are small and may not be as obvious. Yet they affect our lives in significant ways. In order to help others, we must be sensitive to those problems.

How do you discover other people's problems? Sometimes they will tell you. If not, you can also look at the problems you have – you are feeling a lack of meaning in your life, you are feeling stressed, you have money problems, you aren't learning. Recognize that others may be struggling with these same issues.

Sometimes by looking at people, you can intuit what their problems are, even if it's not among your own list of challenges. A single guy or single girl may be worried that they aren't married. Many people have problems with their appearance or their weight.

You may find that many people today have problems that are endemic to our generation. Low self-esteem is epidemic. Use of anti-depressants is at an all-time high.

Draw up a list of the problems that you see people dealing with. By making the effort to focus and ask yourself what people are going through, you learn to understand people.

Once you identify someone's problems, the next step in showing you care is to feel their pain.

How do you do that? Put yourself in someone else's shoes. If you had to beg on the street, how would you feel? If you were having trouble making ends meet every month, how would you feel?

Be particularly open to the pain of people who are going through the same problems that you have personally experienced. The Torah tells you to love a "stranger," a convert, because you were a stranger in Egypt – you know what it was like.

The people that you have the greatest obligation to feel for are the people who have done the most for you, especially your parents, even when their biggest problem may be you!

You need to work at feeling the pain of humanity. First care about the Jews in Israel, but feel also for humanity under tyranny, for people getting AIDS, for people in poverty.

Realize that a person who doesn't have Torah and is lacking real meaning in his life is feeling the pain of that emptiness. This is true even though he doesn't realize what is causing his pain. It was said of one great Torah scholar that he would feel pain seeing a non-Jew not keeping Shabbat, because of what that person was missing out on.

Feeling the pain of others is the first step to motivating yourself to help them. When Moshe, living in Pharaoh's palace, went out to identify with the Jewish people in slavery, it says "he saw their burdens." Rashi translates in his commentary "he focused his eyes and heart to feel pain for them." Only then did he act and stand up for them.

Rabbi Noach Weinberg used to say that "carrying the burden" applies even to carrying the burden for the Almighty. Give G-d at least as much weight as another human being. How would you feel if everyone was destroying the good you gave them? The Rabbis instituted an optional prayer, *Tikkun Hatzot*, for very devout people to wake up in the middle of the night to feel together with the Almighty the burden of G-d's people being in exile and without the Temple.

The first step in helping people is to feel their pain. There are three more 48 Ways to complete the picture. Each one is necessary. If you don't care about people, you won't do a very good job of helping them. If you are able to show that you do care, even if you can't do anything else for them, you help just by making them realize that they are not alone.

Way · 40

Starting the Process of Change

❧ Once you identify a person's problems, help him or her do something about it.

❧ When people have problems, it is often difficult to talk with them directly about their struggle. Instead, "weigh them to the side of merit," by helping them do actions that will make it easier in the long run for them to deal with their problems.

❧ These things can be physical, such as helping them to exercise; medical, such as encouraging them to see a doctor to get the right medication; financial, giving them incentives to do the right thing; or spiritual, helping them to learn Torah which will inspire them.

❧ When you want to help someone, make a plan. Better yet, come up with a few alternate plans.

❧ You can also help yourself solve your own problems by realizing it isn't all or nothing. Get your body moving as a first step to doing more.

The Hebrew text for Way #40 is *Machrio L'kaf Zchut* which translates as, "Weighing Him to the Side of Merit." In the old pre-digital days, storekeepers would weigh items by using a balance scale. The item would be on one side of the scale, the weights on the other. When the weights on one side were equal to the item on the other side, the scale would be balanced. If you put another weight on either side, that side of the scale would go down.

The Rabbis used this metaphor to refer to people. Every person has attributes or character traits that lead him in a good direction and others that lead him the opposite way. When his good qualities and bad qualities are balanced, doing a mitzvah can tip the scale in the direction of good. The Rabbis say: when you want to help a person, find something good you can help him do to tip the scale towards the right side.

This is a crucial step in the process of helping people, the subject of Ways #39–42. Way #39 dealt with caring about people. If you can care about people and feel their pain, you will naturally want to help them to grow and change and overcome their problems.

But how do you do that? We might think that the quickest way to help them would be to sit with them, discuss their problems with them, and give them Torah-based solutions. That would be the next Way, #41, "Giving Inner Clarity: Standing on Truth."

But good luck with that! Imagine you have a friend who is depressed. Depression, as we mentioned in Way #8 – "Living with Joy," is the opposite of joy. It comes from a person looking at his or life as going in a negative direction, with worse and worse things expected to happen in the future. It is a totally debilitating emotion that comes from a negative thought process.

You might think to tell your friend: Come on, snap out of it! Life is great, start thinking positively! G-d loves you, you have a lot to expect in the future! The things that are bothering you can change overnight! Let's work together on doing something to deal with them!

What you just told your friend is the true way to get out of depression. But it isn't likely to work. Your friend is too depressed to make the effort to fight bad thoughts and focus on the positive. He or she may even have a chemical imbalance that makes those bad thoughts overwhelmingly powerful.

But don't give up! The Rabbis say: Weigh your friend to the side of merit. Help him do something positive. Go out with him to a party to get him in a better mood. Learn something with him to get his mind off of his problems. If the depression is severe, help him see a psychiatrist who can prescribe anti-depressant medicine.

None of these solves the problem. But it helps put the person into a state where you can help him solve his problem. By being out and about at the party, he has more energy to work on controlling his negative thoughts. The anti-depressant medicine makes the negative emotions less powerful, so he can start to use his mind to push his thoughts in a more positive direction.

This principle is the one used by all organizations involved in reaching out to Jews today. With the powerful information we can present in programs like our Discovery seminar, we should be able to say to a young Jew: We can prove to you that there is a G-d and the Torah is true! And if the Torah is true, then you have a responsibility to live with it. Get with the program!

Of course we don't do that. When I first came to Aish Hatorah forty years ago, the hook to get me and others to spend time in yeshiva was that it was a free place to stay. And things haven't changed – outreach needs to be highly subsidized. And the goal is to get young people to do some learning. We don't focus on the heaviest issues right away.

All of this is necessary because the body will fight against direct threats to force it to change. So we need to make an end run around the body – get a person into doing positive things that the body won't strongly object to. The result of those positive things will make a person ready to listen and change in the long term.

So if you want to help someone, make a plan. What would lead them in the right direction? Better yet, make five plans and choose the best one.

Although this way is focused on helping others, it can also be a very useful tool to help yourself. An important principle in Judaism is that it isn't all or nothing. None of us is ready to be perfect overnight. It's true, you should be going to *minyan* every day. But start with one or two times a week. You should be using a lot of your spare time for consistent learning. Start with one time a week that you won't change for anything. Work on what your body will allow you to do, and move up step by step.

Way · 41

Giving Inner Clarity: Standing on Truth

❡ To stand him on truth means to show a person the real cause of his or her problems. Problems can only be solved by understanding the reality behind them.

❡ To do this, you have to first believe there is a reality which is different from people's subjective perception.

❡ All our problems have a root in our inability to see the truth. Only when we see the truth can we begin effectively working on solutions to our problems.

❡ Even if a person is unaware of his problems, he is suffering because of them. So be motivated to help even those who don't think they have a problem.

❡ To reach people in the most effective way, work on identifying and showing them their deepest and most fundamental problems, and how they can be solved.

The Hebrew text for Way #41 is *Ma'amido al Ha'emet*, which translates as, "Standing Him Up on Truth." It is the third of a four-part series of Ways that deal with how to help people. Part 1 discussed seeing people's problems and feeling for them. Part 2 was about getting them to do something positive that will make it easier for them to change their situation.

This way addresses deeper solutions. Get people to appreciate the true cause of their situation and use that appreciation to grow and change. The Sages called that "standing someone on truth." Just as a building can only stand solidly if it is built on a strong foundation, a person needs to build his or her life on a foundation of true understanding of themselves, their virtues and their defects.

A look at the nature of human beings can help us understand why this is so difficult, especially in the world today.

As we have mentioned before, the Talmud tells us that an angel taught us all wisdom while we were in our mother's womb. This means that we have the answers to any issue about living in the powerful computer of our mind. Although we forget it all the moment we are born, we are continuously being put in touch with elements of it through education and our experiences.

But to give us free will, G-d joined us with a body that tries to fight against many of these answers. And the body has a powerful lawyer, what we call *yetzer hara*, or "the evil inclination." The *yetzer hara* uses rationalizations, sometimes called "rational lies," to deflect any challenges to what the body desires. To do this, it often uses the wrong ideas we pick up from society, which stick in the mind like computer viruses (We spoke about this idea previously in Way #4 – *Binat Halev*, "Connecting with Your Intuition: Understanding of the Heart").

Because of this, try telling a depressed person that his life could be totally different if he started thinking about his life in a different way. He will have many arguments why his perceptions of his life are correct. Try and tell a secular Jew that there is a G-d and that it can be proved logically. He is likely to answer (without even hearing you out): "You are a fanatic, religion is responsible for most of the evil in the world, science can totally explain everything in the world," and so on.

And if you continue to argue with him, he will bring out the strongest computer virus in the world today, the idea that there is no absolute truth. Everything is a matter of opinion, you have what you think and I have what I think. Forty years ago, in Aish in Jerusalem, we would argue with a small minority of young people who thought that Hitler was right from his perspective, even if from our perspective we don't like what he did. Today the majority argue that truth is subjective. The man who thinks he is a woman should be called "she" not "he." "One man's terrorist is another man's freedom fighter."

So the first step to "standing a person up on truth" is to recommit to the idea of truth. There is a reality about the world that doesn't change because people have different opinions. This is the foundation to understand what is going on in people so you can help them to change.

These realities include: every person needs meaning and needs to feel that he or she is a good person. It also includes that goodness and meaning are objective realities, coming from G-d, not subjective beliefs. (We spoke about this in Way #23 – "Being a Good Person: Having a Good Heart.") The aspects of reality are many, and impact a person's life whether he or she wants to recognize them or not. That is why study of Torah is so important, because it tells us the realities that so much of society today wants to avoid or water down.

Once you have accepted the existence of truth yourself, you can work to stand someone else up on truth. Get them to realize the truth in their situation, so they can deal with it.

For instance: our friend is depressed because he is looking at his life negatively. The reality is that there is nothing in his life that he can't work on changing positively, and G-d will help him to do that. But he doesn't seem to want to look at things that way. Why not? The truth of his situation is that he has internalized a negative image of himself, either from his parents or from his society. So he thinks that nothing he does will succeed.

Standing him up on truth would be to show him that his parents were wrong, and he doesn't have to live his life based on their confusions (a psychologist can show him that). Or it might be to show him that his society has mistaken ideas about success and what is really valuable (a rabbi can show him that).

Or consider two people whose marriage is on the rocks. A marriage counselor might show the husband that his over-concern with work causes him not to pay attention to his wife. And then show the wife that her negative speech towards her husband makes the problem worse.

By showing them the truth about their negative dynamics (usually denied or justified by them at the beginning) the counselor can try to suggest how their marriage can be saved.

In either situation, the depressed person or the rocky marriage, the truth of the situation will vary according to the people involved and the reason for their problems. But there is a truth, a reality, and recognizing it is the key to dealing with the problem.

It isn't easy to get people to see their mistakes. That's why, we said in the last Way, you need to start with helping people get involved in doing something positive. Get the depressed person socializing, learning and possibly on medication. Get the couple to agree to see the marriage counselor. But that only begins the process of healing. People's problems will only be solved totally when you show them the deep roots of their problems, and they see it for themselves.

This goes for all the issues that people have. There is an underlying truth to people's situations, an explanation why they don't believe in G-d, why they are fighting with their spouse, why they are so afraid of failure that they can't take the risks that would better their situation. By connecting them to it, when they are ready to listen, you give them the real tools to change their lives.

The most difficult aspect of helping people is that people are often unaware of what they need to change. Unhappy people will say they are happy, people living in false realities will think they have the truth. In the Guinness Book of World Records, there is a picture of the man with the world's longest fingernails. To make the painful, sustained effort to grow his fingernails to that extent, he must think it is highly meaningful. Yet is it truly meaningful? Will having the world's record really make him a happy and fulfilled person?

To appreciate the need to reach out to those people, and not to leave them unaware, I want to tell a powerful story I heard many years ago from Rav Noach Weinberg. It isn't a real story, but the message is very real and applies to many situations.

Rav Noach asked us to imagine a woman who always wanted to get married and have children. But she married the wrong person, who beat her and left her. She never had the children she wanted, and she was past child-bearing age. From the pain of not getting what she wanted in life, she went insane. In the asylum, she lived with the delusion that she had a new baby every day. She showed it to the doctor every morning.

Rav Noach would ask the question: if you were the doctor in that institution, would you try to get her out of her delusion? Right now she is happy, she has what she wants. If you show her that she has no baby, she will become an unhappy woman in intense pain who can't get what she most wants out of life.

Most people would answer that it is better to keep her happy in her delusion. Some people will say that it is more important she lives with truth, even if she is miserable.

How do you see what the right answer is? Imagine that you are a doctor in that hospital. You had an argument with your wife last night, and you are in a bad mood. When the deluded woman happily shows you her baby on your rounds that morning, you lose it. You say to her: come on, lady, you're making it up, there is no baby there!

What does our intuition tell us about how she would react? She would be angry with the doctor, scream at him, perhaps have a fit (I have run this by psychologists, and they agree that she would react that way unless she was so delusional as to be totally unaware of any reality).

Compare that to a woman in a maternity ward who is holding a real baby. The same grumpy doctor says the same thing. She won't be upset. She will laugh it off, and wonder how that crazy doctor got into the hospital.

Why the difference in reaction? Because the woman with the real baby has a real baby, and the woman with the imaginary baby *knows that she doesn't*. Deep down, she knows the truth and she is as deeply unhappy as she ever was. Her delusion just represents an immense, exhausting effort to cover up what she knows.

A doctor who cares would obviously not tell her the truth in such an insensitive way. He might first "weigh her to the side of merit" by putting her in situations where she can interact with real children. He could counsel her about what she could do with her life even without children. But ultimately, if he cares about her, he has to stand her up in truth, because only then can she deal with the reality of her situation and work to change it.

This example applies on some level to all human beings. The person who has no real meaning in his life has his own imaginary baby. He covers up his lack of meaning by being a workaholic or a party animal, or by being 24/7 on social media. If you point that out to him in a non-caring way, he will get angry at you like the woman with the imaginary baby. But if you care about him, don't accept his protestations that he is happy. Work out how to reach him. A human being without meaning is miserable, and he can't keep up his delusion forever.

The above story gives us the motivation to make the effort to give someone clarity about his or her situation even if he or she doesn't really understand that they have a problem. But even if you want to reach people, it is often very hard to get through to them. Another story, showing how to "stand someone up on truth," is given in the Talmud about Onkelos the convert.

Onkelos became a great Sage and wrote the Aramaic translation of the Torah that is still included along with the Hebrew text of Hebrew *Chumashim*. But he started life as the nephew of the Roman emperor. When he converted, embarrassing his family, the emperor sent soldiers to arrest him. He got in a Torah discussion with the first group of soldiers, and they all ran away and converted to Judaism.

The emperor sent a second group of soldiers with instructions not to get into a Torah discussion with him. He said to them: "In Rome, a minor official carries the torch before a high official, a high official before the duke, the duke before the governor, the governor before the king. Does the king hold the torch for other people? They answered him: Of course, the king doesn't hold the torch for anyone. Onkelos told them: among the Jewish people, we see that G-d went before them in the desert in a pillar of fire to lead them. The second group all ran away and converted.

The emperor sent a third group with instructions not even to talk with him. Onkelos put his hand on the *mezuzah* and asked them: what is this? Overcome with curiosity, they asked him what it was. He said to them: "In the world, the king sits inside and the guards guard outside. But the Jewish people sit inside and the King guards them from outside (as symbolized by the *mezuzah*). The third group also ran away and converted.

As someone who has worked in Jewish outreach for many years, I am amazed and envious. Roman soldiers had to be the roughest human beings around. How did Onkelos manage to convert three groups of these difficult uneducated people?

The answer is that Onkelos spoke to the great truth about their lives. These were Romans. According to our tradition, Rome was descended from our wicked brother Esau. Esau valued power in this world. In Esau's world, the world of Rome, only success counted. Those lower down only existed to serve the ones who succeeded.

Onkelos showed them that life could be different. They didn't have to live with the pain of having to spend their lives serving the king or the general. That realization, spoken by someone who totally believed it, was enough to get through to the roughest human beings and get them to change their lives.

Today, we are still living in Esau's world that arose out of the Roman Empire. Success is still the greatest value of that world. Since most people can't be the richest, most beautiful, or most famous, the pain of trying and not succeeding is around us everywhere. We need to speak truth to the people who are living with the pain of that world, and show them that Judaism looks at the world differently.

The ultimate level of standing a person on truth would be to show them their deeper pain in such a way that they know they must change. Then show them how to face it. May we all care enough about people to learn to speak to them in the way that Onkelos did.

Way · 42

Giving Inner Peace

❡ Inner peace can only come when the body goes along with the soul. Although the soul can never be happy following the desires of the body, the body can be happy going along with the drives of the soul.

❡ The greatest help you can give a person is to help him or her achieve inner peace.

❡ The first step in attaining inner peace is to persuade your body that it will get good things from doing good and meaningful acts. To begin the process, realize that you will gain the positive things you want in life from living with good and meaning.

❡ A higher level of inner peace comes from committing yourself to G-d's cause in a strong enough way that your body takes pleasure in it also. To help others solve their problems, get them committed and involved in that cause.

❡ True greatness, like we see with Abraham, can only come from getting the soul and the body to work together.

The three previous Ways have been dealing with how to help your fellow human beings. First, care about them. Then get them doing something productive. Then help them understand and deal with the issues that are blocking them from solving their problems.
Way #42 "Standing him Up on Peace," – *Ma'amido al HaShalom*

in the Hebrew text – deals with a final way you can help people: giving them inner peace. Don't just help them solve their problems, help them get past their problems to achieve their potential.

Inner peace is something people are desperately looking for – 4 million hits on Google! So attaining inner peace would have to rate as one of the most important things you can do for him or her.

To do this, you need to understand what inner peace is.

As we have mentioned many times, a human being is a soul with a body. The soul is driven for goodness, meaning, and accomplishment. The body wants comfort. Goodness, meaning and accomplishment require discomfort. So the body fights against them. The soul seeks spiritual growth and the life-style connected with it. The body seeks physical gratification and ways to distract the soul from the effort of growth. The result is that every human being starts out with a war between the body and the soul.

Judaism understands that you can't escape from the body. If you try to ignore it or suppress it, like Catholic priests or Hindu mystics do, it takes its revenge in other ways. That is why one of the biggest issues in the church is pedophile priests.

Giving in to the body or even compromising with it is not the answer. A human being is a soul, and the soul will never be content with letting the body do its thing. That's why even a powerful successful dictator like Hitler was an insomniac who had to surround himself with people he could preach to for hours every night. The equally powerful Mao Tse Tung had to take a high dose of sleeping pills that would kill an ordinary person. Their souls were sending them a message that they weren't good people, and kept them from being at peace with themselves.

So how can you successfully fight this war?

The first step is to learn to control the body. Rabbi Noach Weinberg compared it to the case of Siamese twins. You are one of the twins, and you are a respectable sophisticated person. Your twin is disreputable and wants the wrong things. But you can't get rid of him! So what do you do? You have to train him. Teach him that it is in his interest not to shout out at business meetings. Force him to act respectably, even if it is against his nature.

With great effort, the soul – using its power of free will – can work to harness the body and prevent it from interfering with the soul's purposes. It isn't an easy battle, and you won't feel inner peace.

To reach inner peace, you have to get the body on your side. Although the soul can never make peace with the body, the body can make peace with the soul.

We see this on a daily basis if we go to the gym. Gym is something for the soul, which recognizes that a healthy body is necessary to accomplish more in life. At first the body does not want to take the pain. But if you push yourself, and continue to work out, something changes. The body gets to like the feeling of health. If you don't go to the gym for a few days, the body will tell you that you should go back.

This process is really the key to growth. A poor child born in a slum might have a desire to hijack cars, and need to fight his body to overcome it. You don't have that problem, because it is clear to you that it is wrong and counterproductive. Your body doesn't even consider it. But when it comes to white-collar crime, you might be challenged until it becomes clear to you that any dishonesty is wrong. Then you reach a new level of growth. On that issue, you have achieved inner peace.

Our service of G-d works in the same way. For those of us who are *ba'alei teshuva*, it wasn't easy at first to keep Shabbat. The body complained about the soccer game it was missing or the program on TV. But after being committed to keeping Shabbat, and living that way, the body made peace with it. It joined the soul in looking forward to the peace of Shabbat, the nice meals, the family time.

The more you are committed to doing things that are right and meaningful, the more the body will cooperate. The person who is fully committed to living as a soul will be the one who has true inner peace – his enemy has become an ally.

ACHIEVING INNER PEACE – TWO LEVELS

There are two levels to achieving inner peace. The first is to convince the body that it will gain what it is looking for by going along with the soul. That is what happens naturally when we go to gym – the body recognizes that feeling healthy is pleasurable. That is what happens when we keep Shabbos – the body starts enjoying the good food, the family time, the lack of stress. And even when the body hasn't experienced the results yet, you can motivate it by promising it the good results that should come. Tell it: if I commit myself to living a Jewish life, G-d should help me find a good spouse and have a good family.

You can't get inner peace by promising the body things that are not good for the soul. It won't work to say: if I commit some time to learning Torah, it's OK to spend the rest of my time on video games. The soul will still object. But the things that the body likes that the soul can also appreciate will bring you to peace.

The Torah teaches us this with regard to Abraham, the founder of the Jewish people. By the time G-d first spoke to Abraham, he had already accomplished a lot. He had come to the realization of G-d in a world that believed only in idol worship. He went out to reach out to others, even breaking their idols to teach them that idol worship was wrong. Nimrod, the powerful king of Abraham's birthplace Shinar, presented him with a choice of bowing down to his idols or getting thrown into a fire. Abraham chose death and was only saved by a miracle.

When Abraham was seventy-five, G-d told him to leave everything he had been doing up to then and leave the comforts and protection of family to go to Israel to start the process of bringing the world back to G-d. Our tradition understands that G-d was testing Abraham – would he be willing to take this extra step into the unknown? As an incentive to pass the test, G-d promises him children, money, and fame.

But why promise him anything? Wouldn't it have been a greater test without the incentive? And wouldn't Abraham, who was already willing to be thrown into the fire for G-d, have been willing to do this without the incentive?

The Torah is telling us that the incentive was necessary. Up to this point, Abraham had been a good man, doing major things. But he hadn't taken on responsibility for the world. To achieve that greater level, he would need his body to go along with him. To die for G-d, as he was willing to do when challenged by Nimrod, doesn't require the body's agreement – the soul can force the body not to get in the way for the short space of time it takes to die. But to live for G-d, on a constant basis, takes constant effort, and the soul needs help from the body. Children, money, fame, were things the body and the soul could agree on. Even though it would seem that money and fame are for the body alone, the soul can want them also. Ask the leader of any organization that has a positive spiritual goal but needs money and name recognition to achieve its purposes.

Bribing the body to cooperate with the soul is the first level of inner peace. An even higher level is to get the body totally behind the soul's purpose. The body has the ability to want goodness and meaningfulness. When you have a cause that the soul and body both agree on, with no reservations, you have achieved the ultimate in inner peace.

Of course there are many false causes, and a false cause won't give you inner peace. The soul will not go along with saving the whales as an ultimate cause, or even global warming. Islamic fundamentalists think they have an ultimate cause, but it doesn't satisfy them – that is why they often seem to be such angry people.

This higher level was reached by Abraham more than 60 years after the Almighty first spoke to him, when G-d told him to bring his son Isaac as a sacrifice. What he was being asked to do was totally against what G-d had promised him before. It would destroy everything he had been striving to do, to bring the world to G-d by having his son take over his mission. Yet he got up early and saddled his own donkey in zealousness to fulfill the word of G-d. The body went along with the soul totally, even though there was nothing in it for the body except for the ultimate meaning of doing G-d's will.

STANDING OTHERS ON PEACE

From the understanding of how to obtain inner peace, we can appreciate that the most powerful way to help your fellow human beings is to help them towards this same goal. There are different levels of this: to introduce non-observant Jews to Judaism will give them more meaning and some inner peace. The more Torah becomes part of their lives, the more peace they will have. Helping them to get married and start families, and making them part of a Jewish community, will add more peace to their lives.

But the most powerful way to bring inner peace to others is to get them totally committed to G-d's cause. Help them work on bringing the Jewish people back to G-d, or helping the Jewish people in Israel, or being Torah scholars and teaching Torah to others. A person truly involved in these things will have no time for the pettiness of the body and its desires.

By giving a person a mission and a responsibility, you can totally change his or her life. The Talmud gives an example. When one of the great rabbis died, Rabbi Yehuda HaNasi asked in his Beit Midrash: does this rabbi have any children that we can honor? His students said: He has one son, and every prostitute in the city knows him. Rabbi Yehuda went looking for him on the bad side of town, found him with a lady on each arm, walked over and gave him *semicha*, rabbinical ordination. The young man said to himself: I'm a rabbi now, I have to learn. He went back with Rabbi Yehuda to the Beit Midrash and became a great rabbi himself. His new level of responsibility was enough to allow his soul to conquer his body.

Having inner peace is the key to achieving greatness. A great leader, like Abraham, or a great Torah scholar, can't achieve that greatness while constantly fighting the body. The energy to really accomplish comes from having body and soul work together.

By involving a person in Torah learning and real meaning in life, you are guiding him or her on a path to greatness. You yourself become great by doing it, because his or her accomplishments become your accomplishments as well. Achieve your own inner peace by giving peace to others.

Way · 43

Desiring to Learn

❡ To get the most out of learning, the body needs to be involved also.

❡ To do this, you have to learn what fascinates you. Your body is drawn to information that it feels is relevant to your life.

❡ Use that awareness when learning Torah: the Almighty Creator of the Universe gave us "Torat Chaim, "Instructions for Living," so it must all be relevant to our lives.

❡ Different types of Torah take different skills to find the pleasure. Learn to focus on what is fascinating about each type.

❡ The Rabbis say "A person should always learn what his heart desires" – use that as an entry point to fulfill your responsibility to know all of Torah.

The 48 Ways starts out with *B'Talmud*, the importance of learning. Learning is the most central tool in Judaism for gaining a relationship to G-d. G-d gave us His Torah, His instructions for living. It is our most direct way to connect with the purpose of life and what G-d wants from us. It is the key to get in touch with the knowledge that the angel put into the computer of our mind.

But there is one problem with learning. The drive to learn starts out as a spiritual drive from the soul. Since it takes effort to learn, the body does not necessarily desire to do it. Although observant

Jews, following Jewish law, will make sure to make time for learning, it can be an exhausting body-soul struggle to learn consistently.

The Hebrew term for Way #43 is *Mityashev Libo B'talmudo*, literally "Absorbing his Heart in his Studies." It is the first of a series of Ways on the techniques of learning. It pushes us to take a step further in developing our Torah study. To get the most out of learning, we need to get the body desiring to learn also.

To do that, you have to work out what information motivates you, and why.

BECOMING FASCINATED BY LIFE

Plenty of people are news junkies. They find what is going on in the world fascinating. That is why CNN, Fox, and Sky are so successful. What is Trump going to do today? Will the Democrats win their fight against him and get rid of him? Will Europe finally do something about terrorist attacks? That's today's news – tomorrow's news will be totally different and just as fascinating.

What is that fascination? We sense that we will understand something more about life from what we see. It can be learning about people and what they do, or the fight between good and evil, or the insanity of the world, or some information that will change our lives for the better.

Most of what we think we will learn is an illusion. Although sometimes we do pick up important information, most of the time it is just the background noise of living in the world, where today's crisis is tomorrow's old news. But while we are in the middle of it, it becomes easy to read and learn about it.

This natural fascination with life is something we can work on improving. To start, we can hone in on what fascinates us. Rabbi Weinberg used to point out that we all have an inner Geiger counter that tells us where relevant information might be found. If someone tells you how many bricks there are in a particular building, the Geiger counter says – not interested. But we can listen longer to a geologist telling us about the different types of rocks in the world. But not too much longer, unless we are studying it at university. We might have an even greater attention span listening to someone who really knows about plants, although we would get tired of that soon also. But when it comes to animals, we can read books about "elephant whisperers" and people who lived with lions. And when someone tells us about people, we never get tired of it – that is why People magazine sells out and why we read novels.

What sets off the Geiger counter? A perception, often subconscious, about how relevant this information is to our lives. Bricks in a building isn't relevant at all. The geology of rocks is a window into G-d's creation – we feel it has meaning, even though we have no idea what it is. Plants are closer to us than rocks, animals than plants. People and information about them are the most relevant of all.

Learn to be sensitive to your Geiger counter, because it is the starting point for your body to be interested in the pursuit of wisdom.

Torah learning is harder to be interested in than secular information. The body creates more resistance. But you can work to get the body into it by focusing on the fact that this is the real information about life from the Ultimate source. Tell the body – this is from G-d, it must be deep. These are the real secrets of what life is about. The Almighty Creator of the world wants me to know this – He wouldn't want me to know it if it wasn't important.

BECOMING FASCINATED BY TORAH

When we start to learn, certain parts of the Torah will speak to us more than other parts. Discover what aspects of Torah are more naturally interesting to you. On Yom Kippur night, when it was important to keep the Kohen Gadol awake all night, people would read to him from the Book of Daniel, which deals with when the *Mashiach* is coming, and the Book of Job, which deals with the meaning of suffering. Stories are easier to be interested in at first than difficult Talmudic discussions on Jewish law. The stories of Chumash and Tanach with the Midrash deal more directly with people and can be used to turn yourself on to learning.

For more complicated learning, use the body's natural appreciation for a puzzle. This appreciation is why we enjoy Crossword puzzles or chess. You can use it to get involved with Torah learning also. The Rabbis intentionally set down important principles for living in collections of wisdom like *Pirke Avos* as puzzles to be unlocked, so that you would be involved in figuring out the meaning. Be fascinated at discovering: what is the obvious question here? How could they say that this is true when the life I see in front of me seems so different? Doesn't this idea seem so obvious that they shouldn't have to tell it to me?

It takes time for most people, but the style of the Talmud – questions upon questions upon questions – makes learning into a complex puzzle. To the true Talmud scholar, there is no greater pleasure.

For many people today, a taste of mysticism helps motivate them to learn. Although the body of Kabbalah can only be learned by someone who has mastered all the basics of Torah, Kabbalistic insights can motivate people to see that the Torah is a connection to something deeper and greater. Books like "The Way of G-d," by Rabbi Moshe Chaim Luzzatto, or the Tanya, by the first Lubavitcher Rebbe, can serve as gateways to wisdom.

The Rabbis say "A person should always learn what his heart desires." Although we have a responsibility to work on knowing all the Torah, by starting with what we are most interested in learning, we can develop the energy to learn so much more.

Way · 44

The Key to Unlocking your Mind: Asking and Answering

❡ An angel taught your mind all the Torah. But you need to use tools to access that information.

❡ Asking the right questions and answering them are the first steps to expanding your knowledge of any part of wisdom.

❡ Variations of "what," "how," and "why" are questions you can use for almost any subject.

❡ When you ask your mind for answers, the mind will retrieve what it knows. But it also comes up with the wrong information you have been taught or have acquired during your life. With practice, you can learn to separate correct answers from false ones.

❡ The Talmud, the foundation book for advanced Jewish study, is a complex user's guide to the potentials of asking and answering.

In the previous Way, "Desiring to Learn," the Rabbis gave a first technique for learning Torah: find out what interests you. From now until the end of the 48 Ways, they continue to give more techniques for learning. Although all the 48 Ways are necessary to grow in Torah, there are specific techniques to expand your mind and make use of the incredible wisdom G-d gave us.

Way #44 – *Sho'el U'meishiv*, meaning "Asking and Answering," is the most famous learning tool in Judaism, because it is the tool on which the entire Talmud is based. As has been reported in the media, South Koreans have picked up on Talmud study. It isn't because they are interested in G-d and His laws, the subject of the Talmud, but because they appreciate the immense value for their own lives of the powerful thinking tool the Talmud demonstrates. So besides giving the basis for Jewish law, the Talmud will also be responsible for some Samsung apps.

The reason why this thinking tool is necessary is that G-d has given us a mind that is a computer loaded with all the important information we need for living. As we mentioned before, we lose touch with that computer at birth, and get reconnected by what we learn throughout life.

But what we learn at any one time only connects us to a small part of what we have in that computer. What we learn in one place, on one subject, is not necessarily connected in our minds with what we have learned on other subjects, even related ones. The tool to expand and connect with the much vaster information we have is to learn to ask the right questions and access our own answers. Through knowing how to use this tool, we take ideas we have learned and connect them into broad patterns of interlocking ideas that help us understand life and use our wisdom in the best way.

ASKING

The best way to show how this works is by example. Take the concept of "love" which we have already discussed numerous times in the 48 Ways.

We all know that love is a positive quality. But what is love? We have already given a definition in previous Ways – "love is an emotion of pleasure that comes from appreciating the virtues of another human being and identifying them with those virtues." But if you hadn't already heard the answer from us, asking the question "what is love?" would start your mind thinking about a potential answer.

Once you have the answer (or have learned it from a source), you can go to the next question: How do I know that this definition is the true one? And another question: Why is it important to know this definition? And another question: How do I put this definition into practice?

The questions "what," "how" and "why" are tools to open almost any subject.

But there are more advanced questions that can be asked also. In the Talmud, they are called *kashes*, "hard things," usually questioning apparent contradictions. For instance, if love is appreciating virtues, why don't I love the world's greatest rabbi more than I love my mother or my child, who probably have less virtues? Or another *kasha*: If love is such a pleasure, why don't we make more effort to expand the number of people we love in order to get more pleasure?

ANSWERS

Questions get you started thinking. But the greatest benefit from using the tool of questions comes when you are able to come to your own answers. Since most of the time, you don't have a knowledgeable rabbi around to ask, you need to learn to answer your own questions.

How do you do that?

The first principle to answering is to recognize that you have answers. If you ask your mind a question, it will give you back information. It is true that we start out with very little control of the process. But you don't really know how you use your hand, yet somehow your thought that you want to move it causes the brain to make the right nerves and muscles move. And, through practice, you can use your hand in more and better ways. In the same way, your mind also "listens" to you, and you can train yourself to get better at it.

Not all answers that your mind gives you are true. The answer it gives you can be true information, coming from understandings of life you have picked up through your own education and experiences. Or it can be wrong information, from the mistaken information and computer viruses that you have picked up along the way in life. The desires of the body, using the lawyer that we call the "*yetzer hara*," will often push the wrong answers on us. So you have to judge the information the mind gives you, often by asking further questions, and learn to distinguish true answers from prejudices and mistaken information.

To give an example of how our thinking process works, let's take the questions we raised earlier.

Ask yourself: what is the definition of love? It is definitely an emotion. But what emotion? Your mind may come up with previous definitions you heard: Love is never having to say you're sorry. Or: love is giving. But you can ask yourself *kashes* on those answers: don't I have to say I'm sorry to my wife, even though I love her? Don't I give to people because I think it is the right thing to do, even if I don't love them?

So what is it? If you keep working on it, you will get closer to the true definition.

If you already have a definition (like the one we gave earlier), ask questions on it. How do I know that the definition we gave is true? An answer: Because if I ask myself why I love any person, I will always answer to myself that I love that person because he or she is good or kind or intelligent, not because he or she is lazy or prejudiced. But then I can ask a *kasha*: If love is because of perceiving virtues, why don't I love the greatest rabbi more than my family? An answer: Because it is real to me that the virtues of my family members are fundamental parts of their nature, and I don't really know the greatest rabbi in more than a superficial way.

Often, the mind will give you different possible answers and you have to sort them out. For example: Why is it important to know this definition? Your mind might answer that it isn't important, because I love who I love and I don't love who I don't love. That's what I feel and thinking doesn't change feelings (this is a common computer virus). Or it might answer that, since I speak about love all the time, and others use the word, it is important to know what I/they mean (a partial answer). Or it might answer: if I know what causes me to love people, I can look for virtues and love more people, and even appreciate the people I do love more (a deeper, more useful answer).

When you have an answer that seems correct to you, you can still ask questions to go further. If I accept that love comes from seeing virtues, and that loving people is a good thing (it is actually a mitzvah, "love your neighbor as yourself"), how do I put it into practice? Start looking at people and writing down their virtues. Practice seeing the virtues in people.

Rav Noach Weinberg used to say that any of the 48 Ways can be turned into questions. From Way #1, *B'Talmud*, "study," comes the question – how much time is it worth spending in order to learn how to love people, and when should I schedule that time in my day? From Way #2, "Listening to Life's Messages" (*Shmiat HaOzen*) – what is a virtue, and why does it cause you to love someone (Hint: virtues are aspects of G-dliness in a person)? From Way #4, "The Understanding of the Heart" (*Binat Halev*): Do I love my mother or my children more, and why? And so on.

What you have done by using this process is that you have taken a single idea and expanded it into a wide matrix. If you are a teacher, you have at least one class to teach, maybe a seminar. If you aren't a teacher, you have a whole set of ideas about life that have been activated.

It isn't easy to learn the process. When you come up with an answer, you have to check that it fits in with what else you know. Check out your answers with your teachers, especially at first. But if you work on it, you gain in skill, similar to learning to ride a bicycle or drive a shift car. The mind learns to do naturally what was once difficult for it.

Once you have developed the skill, you can hear a question and make a judgment: I can answer this; I need more information; if I think more about it I can come up with the answer; I have a partial understanding but not a total answer; I don't have a clue.

Ultimately, to really develop the skill of thinking, you need to learn the Talmud. If Koreans can learn Talmud for the sake of Samsung apps and better Hyundai cars, you can learn it also to improve your service of G-d and your ability to lead a meaningful life.

The next four Ways give further steps in this process of mind expansion.

Way · 45

The Key to Creativity:
Hearing and Adding On

❡ "Asking and Answering" (Way #44) deals with tools for taking a subject and analyzing it more deeply. Way #45 provides the tools to apply information on one subject in order to learn about other subjects.

❡ Rabbi Noach Weinberg used key words to do this: conclusion, implication, derivation, corollary, consequence. Another way to do this is to use Google as a model for our mind's ability to search its data-base and connect seemingly unrelated concepts.

❡ When you have a definition for love, use it to examine other areas where the word "love" is used – the use of "love" in secular music, "I love my job," love of Communism or other political philosophies.

❡ Using your mind this way is a key to creativity, to discovering new insights from many different places in your mind.

❡ Always check out your answers using the Torah you have learned, the feedback of rabbis and fellow-students, and your own ability of "Binat Halev," checking with your intuition.

The previous Way, #44, was "Asking and Answering." Asking the right questions and answering them is the basic technique of analytical reasoning. Through it, you can understand any subject in depth, whether in Torah or outside of Torah.

Way #45 in Hebrew, is *Shome'ah U'mosif*, "He Hears and Adds to It." It deals with the technique of taking an idea and building on it by connecting it to related ideas and using it to understand them. Through it, you can take one part of Torah and use it to gain insight into other parts of Torah or even secular affairs. It is the key to creativity, which involves connecting different ideas to see things in a totally new way.

As we mentioned before in previous Ways, G-d gave us a computer programmed with all wisdom about living. We are born out of touch with it, but get in touch with different parts of it through education and experience. The more Torah learning we have, the more we are in touch with our inner information.

But this information we have gotten in touch with is logged in our mind in different places under different programs. We have a program for "Wisdom about love and marriage," another one for "Wisdom about making a living," another one for "Wisdom about the situation of the world today." These programs don't necessarily connect with each other. Learning how to connect them is the subject of this Way. Connecting the programs would be what is meant by the phrase "thinking out of the box" – the box in our mind that we have stored the particular program we are dealing with at the moment.

When Rabbi Noach Weinberg taught this Way, he used certain key words as tools to get deeper and more "out-of-the box" understanding: Conclusion, implication, derivation, corollary, consequence. It is hard to use these tools today (and was hard for us back then, 40 years ago).

As another approach, we can use the tool we all learn from Google. Use key words to search the data bank of your mind.

For example, in the previous Way we talked about the word "love." We showed how an analysis of the word "love" starts from the definition: "an emotion of pleasure from perceiving the virtues in another human being." From that definition, we could deepen our understanding of who we love, why we love them, how we can learn to love them better, how we can expand the number of people we love.

But can we expand our knowledge of other subjects by using our definition of love? Try googling "Love secular music" (you'll get over 27,800,000 hits). Or google it in your mind – you won't find a million pieces of information, but you will find a lot of songs hanging around in your mind that talk about love. "Love was here and now it's gone," "Where did our love go?" are still titles stuck in my mind from the old pre-yeshiva days. But what "love" are they talking about? It can't be love that comes from perceiving virtues, because if you really perceived the person's virtues, why would the love go? People don't easily change their virtues. Your love of your parents or children doesn't just disappear!

Asking the question "What do they mean by love?" is using the Way of "He asks and answers." And by using it on the songs you remember, you can easily see that the love they are talking about is the physical desire between a man and a woman that the secular world calls love.

And you can go on from there to a deeper analysis of Western society: What does it mean that multi-billion dollar industries are based on a false concept of love? What does that tell us about the craziness of the world we are living in? How does that affect our own ability to love our spouses in a world where so much effort goes into presenting a false idea of love? And how do we go about countering it in our own lives?

All this, and lots more, comes from using your mind to connect two previously somewhat unrelated concepts. What if you try to do that with concepts that are more unrelated? Try googling "love work" (over 7 billion hits!).

Obviously there is some relationship. That is because people will say they "love their job." Why is that? If love is perceiving virtue, what virtue does an accountant perceive in his work? The intellectual challenge? Or does he love the money or the status? Or the chance to be together with coworkers he likes in the office?

Someone who has learned Pirke Avos would google in his mind that the Sage Shemaiah says "Love work, hate positions of authority." What did he mean by saying "love work"? Since he was talking about all work, it can't be directed at a particular job. He meant to appreciate the virtue of supporting yourself and your family, of not depending on others, of not having to seek a position of authority to get respect and power by lording it over others.

From this, you can ask yourself: Do I love my work? And if I don't love the actions I have to do every day or the people I do it with, can I still learn to love and appreciate the fact that it provides me the money to take care of my family, learn Torah, give charity and support my community?

And what if you do the google search on concepts that seem totally unrelated, like "love Islamic fundamentalism" (believe it or not 1,120,000 hits on Google).

So what can you discover? The #1 article that comes up on Google is "The left's love affair with Islam." Using "he asks and answers," ask yourself the question: Why do leftists love Islam? Google your mind for what you know about Islamic fundamentalism. It can't be that Western leftists love Islam because they love the "virtues" of Islamic fundamentalists such as their attitude toward women, their attitude toward homosexuals, their support of violent jihad – all of those go against left-wing beliefs. They don't love religious beliefs when religious Jews or Christians have them. So what do they love? It must be that they love the fact that Islamic fundamentalists hate the Western society that the left-wing hates. From this can come a deeper understanding of what is happening in the self-hating Western society that so many Jews have bought into. Through that understanding, we can work out a better idea of how to get them out of it.

Using this process, you can vastly increase the amount of knowledge you have on anything you consider important. It isn't easy, it takes practice. The more Torah information you have, the better you will be able to do it. And since our judgment is impacted by our desires, and from the computer viruses that we have picked up from bad education and society, mistakes are common. Especially at the beginning, you need to check out your understandings with others, and test them with other information that you have.

Rabbi Weinberg used to point out that the greatest punishment in prisons is to put people into solitary confinement. It isn't something we would wish on ourselves or others. But a person who is in touch with the abilities of the mind and how to use them, and knows some wisdom, will never have to fear being alone. There are great treasures in your mind waiting to be uncovered.

Way · 46

Learning in Order to Teach

¶ To really understand an idea, think out how you would teach it.

¶ "Learning in order to teach" gets us out of the comfort zone of seeing only what is immediately relevant to us. By having to consider the viewpoint of another person, we expand our own understanding.

¶ Use this as a tool for any of your Torah learning – what would a secular person, a person of a different age or gender, a person who had very different experiences than you – need to learn about this particular idea or story? What questions would they have?

¶ Focusing on how to teach something also helps you to become more organized in your thinking and see the deeper potential of any subject.

¶ It isn't necessary to have real students to do this. But once you have imagined how to teach students, you will have more confidence to actually go out and find those students.

In Way #12 – "Growth through Teaching: The Questioning of Students," we discussed the importance of teaching. Teaching is a responsibility. If you know the cure for cancer and don't share it with others, you are responsible for the deaths that result. If you know wisdom and don't teach it to people who need it, you are responsible for the ways in which they suffer from the lack of that wisdom.

We also said that teaching was an important way to gain wisdom for yourself. Students' questions, and the need to clarify when you teach, gives the teacher a much deeper understanding of whatever he or she is teaching.

Way #46, *Lomed Al M'nat L'Lamed*, "He Learns in Order to Teach," focuses on a different benefit that comes from teaching. As part of a series of techniques of learning Torah, it provides an important new technique. To really understand an idea, think out how you would teach it, even if you aren't going to teach it now.

To understand the value of this, we need to go back to our model of the mind as a computer. To expand our wisdom, we need to get in touch with the deeper answers in our computer. The 48 Ways has already taught us the two tools that form the basis of the Talmud – "Asking and Answering," and "Hearing and adding on." Using these tools will offer greater understanding of any subject.

Yet even when we use these tools, we can be limited by the pain it takes to think (Remember Henry Ford, quoted in Way #13 – "Searching your Mind for Wisdom with Deliberateness" – "*Thinking is the hardest work there is*"). So even the person who is learning Torah, who is committed to thinking, has his comfort zone limitations. Our natural tendency is to think within that comfort zone, and resist going outside of it.

We can see how this process works if we think of daily experiences. When we are giving a report to people in our office, we are likely to focus on what we want to say. It is more of an effort to think about what they need or will want to hear. When we are trying to teach our children about life, our comfort zone is to want to tell them what we think they need to know. We are less likely to think about how they are feeling and how they will respond to what we are telling them.

"Learning in order to teach" is a key tool to help us out of that comfort zone. In the above examples, it would involve imagining to ourselves, before we speak, what our audience will be thinking and asking, and modifying our presentation accordingly. Or imagining what our kids are thinking (if that's possible!) and teaching what we feel they need to know based on that understanding.

Getting out of this comfort zone can impact all our Torah learning. For instance, when you are learning Jewish law, you may be content to just learn what to do in your daily life. Extra effort would be needed to ask why the law is this way, something that may require more deep thinking and is not always discussed directly in the book you are studying. But if you imagine teaching a less committed student – who will want to know the reason – you will be forced to make an effort to find out. You will push yourself to look into other sources, to ask your teachers, or just to question your intuition. You will grow in your own wisdom from asking and finding the answer.

This doesn't just apply to laws that need to be clarified. It can work for any aspect of Torah.

For example: You may be studying the weekly Torah portion and come to *Parshat* Chaye Sara, where Abraham sends out his servant Eliezer to find a wife for his son Isaac. Eliezer succeeds through a great miracle in finding Isaac a wife to continue the family line of the Jewish people.

An older married person learning this story might focus on how the Almighty takes care of his holy ones to ensure the future of the Jewish people. He might pay more attention to how Eliezer fulfills his mission, and ask if it was right to set up the sort of test that he did – "if a girl comes out and does [x-y-z], that will be the one." He might wonder at the fact that the Torah considers it important to write about Eliezer telling over his whole story even though it has already told us the story – as the Rabbis say "More beautiful is the chatter of the servants of the forefathers than the Torah of their children." His comfort zone is to focus on the aspects of the story that seem immediately relevant to him.

But if that married man thinks how he would teach it to young unmarried men (even though he isn't teaching anyone at present), he will become aware that the standards Abraham set for Eliezer and the test that Eliezer set for Rebecca can help them understand what they should be looking for in a wife. He would face the questions that might come up – why is family so important that Abraham sent Eliezer to choose a wife from his family, who are idol worshippers, rather than looking around for someone closer to home who can be checked out more? Why did Eliezer choose to test for the quality of kindness, and didn't seem to care what Rebecca believed in? How can the Torah present a marriage arranged by others as a proper thing – what if Isaac didn't like Rebecca or Rebecca didn't like Isaac?

From looking into these issues, provoked by the needs and questions of potential students, he can get deeper insights into life. These insights, which he would otherwise have missed, can help his own marriage, as well as help him to advise others.

Asking deeper moral questions is often outside our comfort zone. If we have not had serious suffering in our lives, we may not be strongly motivated to ask the question: why do good people suffer? But thinking of teaching a person who has suffered greatly will force us to make the effort to work out the issue. The understandings we come to will help us appreciate better what we see happening around us in the world, and will give us a better foundation to deal with suffering if we experience it later.

Focusing on how you would teach something also helps you in other ways. You have to organize the subject, find the important principles, understand how the different ideas you would teach fit together. This preparation will help you better understand what you are learning, and discover new and deeper insights.

When you teach someone, you have to make the subject interesting. By thinking how to make a somewhat dry part of Torah interesting to someone else, you might discover for yourself why it is really exciting.

All of us have the capability and responsibility to teach some students the important wisdom we have discovered from Torah and from our life experiences. But don't think you need students waiting for you. We can imagine different types of students and what their questions would be. The answers we come up with will increase our own understanding and give us the confidence to seek real students. In fact, it may be that working out those answers is what the Almighty is waiting for so He can send us the real students who need our answers.

Way · 47

Bringing Learning into the Real World: Learning in Order to Do

᠅ G-d gave us a Torah that we call "Torat Chaim," "Instructions for Living." That means that we need to apply Torah in our lives, not just keep its wisdom in our minds.

᠅ The basic principle behind the revolutionary Jewish concept of mitzvot is that wisdom will only change us if we force the body to do something about it.

᠅ The details of Jewish law are immediately applicable to our lives, but other aspects of Torah need to be clarified and understood more deeply before they can be applied.

᠅ With anything that you learn, try to find at least one way to put it into practice.

᠅ Judaism isn't all or nothing. If you learn an important idea, and are not ready to do anything about it now, make a time on your calendar for when you will.

Way #46 – "Learning in Order to Teach," gave us a tool to get outside our comfort zone in thinking. It taught us to look at things through the eyes of a person we are teaching. The goal of Way #47, *Lomed Al M'nat LaAsot*, "Learning in Order to Do," is to remove us from an even greater comfort zone. Even when we are committed to learning, we still need to go a step further by actually applying what we learn and making life changes.

The Jewish understanding of Torah is that it is G-d's instructions for living. Everything in it is meant to give us greater awareness of how to live our lives. So to learn Torah without doing what it teaches is a form of cognitive dissonance. If I know that the infinite, all-knowing, all-powerful, and all-good Creator is telling me to do something, I must be crazy not to do it.

Yet, because we are souls in bodies, we all have a bit of that craziness. There is a gap between what we think and understand, and what we choose to do about it.

We can see this in humanity if we look at the two major religions that originated from Judaism – Christianity and Islam. Each took a tremendous amount of their basic ideology from Judaism, and each has over a billion adherents. But each one rejected the most crucial, transformational element of Judaism – mitzvot, acts that require putting the ideas of Judaism into practice. Christianity rejected them entirely, Islam kept some but not most of them. They didn't reject this by accident. The ideas were fine, but when it came to doing, the body jumped up and said: don't go that far.

Rejection of mitzvot increased the popularity of those religions, but limited their ability to change their followers in a deeper way. The wisdom and laws of the Torah are a package deal. The actions that come from the Torah's wisdom are what causes us to change permanently.

So, in order to get the full value of G-d's Torah, we have to commit ourselves to doing what we learn.

But that isn't enough. To do what we learn, we have to take our learning to the point of working out clear actions. And here is where the body tries to keep us in our comfort zone. It is OK to learn ideas, but it resists the next step: thinking about what to do because of those ideas. The purpose of the Way of "Learning in Order to Do" is to get us to that step, just past our comfort zone.

"Learning in Order to Do" means to take what you learn, work out what you should do about it and then do it. There are a number of different levels in how this works.

The first is the easiest. Jewish law is a series of actions. Say the *shema* two times a day at certain times. Pray three times a day. Say blessings before and after meals. When you are learning a book of Jewish law, much of the information is immediately applicable.

The next level up is responsibilities that you know need to be done, but you have to work out how to do them. We know we have a mitzvah to learn Torah. But what do we learn, and how much time do we spend on it? We know we have a mitzvah to give charity, but how much do we give, and to whom, and in what way?

The key to dealing with these is to learn the details, see how they apply to your life, and make a plan. To work out how to apply the mitzvah of Torah learning, learn the "Laws of Talmud Torah" from the Rambam, or speak to your local rabbi. Then decide how much time you have, and what you think would be most productive to learn. Then make a learning plan for yourself and stick to it. To carry out the mitzvah of giving charity, learn the laws of giving charity from the Rambam or from books in English, and decide how much you have to give, and who you are going to give it to. Then give it.

A higher and more difficult level deals with things we know are meaningful, but aren't clear what to do to put them into practice. Many of the 48 Ways fall into that category. Being humble, having joy, loving people, feeling the pain of others – all 48 Ways – are complex ideas that require much effort over a long period of time to fully and properly execute. "Learning in Order to Do" would tell us to come up with at least one action you can take that is based on each of the 48 Ways. For humbleness, think of a cause you would like to be more committed to, and look for a way to volunteer. For joy, decide to say *Modeh Ani*, "thank you G-d for keeping me alive," every morning with joy. For loving people, make a list of the virtues of one person you don't normally pay attention to, and do something for him or her. For caring for others, take one person and notice the problems he or she has, and do something to show you empathize. And so on.

The stories of the Torah are also meant to teach us about living. How do you apply them? For instance, what does the story of the life of Abraham teach us? We have to understand and clarify more. Why did G-d tell us the story of Abraham? Because He made a permanent covenant with Abraham to make his children chosen people. Why did He do that? Because Abraham took on the responsibility to change the world by bringing people to G-d. So we should do that too! But how? What do we see Abraham doing? We see that he took in guests. That is at least one action we can do. Decide to invite a non-*frum* friend for Shabbat. Then actually do it.

Obviously there are many more things you can learn from

Abraham, and other actions you can choose. But "Learn in Order to Do" teaches that whatever you are learning about, try to express its essence in at least one action.

The basic principle of this Way is: 1 – Clarify what you learned. 2 – Figure out a way to apply it. 3 – Carry through to action.

Realize that you will have a crisis of confidence in yourself if you don't carry through what you learn. We expect other people to live according to their ideals, and we need to as well. When you do carry through with what you believe, you gain tremendous confidence. You know that your decisions mean something.

It can seem like an immense and scary task to put all your learning into practice. You can't do it all at once. But Judaism isn't all or nothing. The great Rabbi Hillel said "If not now, when?" He meant that, if you see something you need to do, don't put it off, do it now. Rabbi Noach Weinberg added: Hillel also meant to say that, if you aren't going to do it now, at least make a plan for when you will do it, and put it on your calendar.

Way · 48

Fighting a Closed Mind:
Making your Teacher Wise

❡ "Making One's Teacher Wise" is the antidote to the closing of the mind that comes when we hear something we totally disagree with.

❡ When you totally disagree with what someone said, ask yourself: is there any way he might actually be right?

❡ Having a teacher helps you hear things you may disagree with at first. If you have received wisdom from someone, it is hard to say that what they are saying now is totally worthless.

❡ The Rabbis say: "Who is wise? The one who learns from every person." Even ordinary people have the possibility of teaching you something true that you may not want to hear.

❡ Don't blindly reject or accept what your teacher says. If you disagree, try to "make him wise." You will both understand more afterwards.

A number of years ago, we took a group of secular university students to Israel on our Jerusalem Fellowships program. One of the presentations was by Gila Manolson, a star teacher who writes well-received books about relationships. One of her special subjects, and the subject of her class to the students, was the prohibition in Jewish law of men and women becoming physically involved before marriage. She teaches about it in a very with-it way, with plenty of modern-day true stories that show the negative results of people becoming involved too quickly.

It is a hard subject for secular young men (secular young women are more likely to understand and agree with it). But I particularly remember one young man who stormed out of the class saying in a loud voice "This is the most illogical presentation I have ever heard!"

I had been listening to her presentation, and what she said didn't seem to me illogical at all. But to him, it not only went against his desires, which was to be expected, but it seemed to him to go totally against his mind. So there was no way he could expect himself to even consider it.

Way #48 – *Machkim et Rabo*, "Making One's Teacher Wise," teaches us how to fight against the closing of the mind that comes when we hear something we totally disagree with.

For a secular young man, it could be something like the above example. But it could happen when a rabbi advises a young man or woman to go to yeshiva or seminary instead of taking a job right after university. Or a career counselor tells you that being a doctor is not for you. Or a marriage counselor tells you that criticizing your husband is destroying your marriage. Or your friend tells you that working overtime to make more money at your job is not worth the effect it is having on your family.

In each case, the rabbi, counselor, or friend might be wrong. Every human being makes mistakes. But what if they are right? When we are totally convinced about something, we won't even consider another possibility.

"Making One's Teacher Wise" confronts that mental closure. When you totally disagree with what someone said, that is the time to ask yourself: is there any wisdom in what I am hearing, is there any way that he/she might actually be right?

To open yourself to that question, first look at whether the other person has some credentials to say what he or she is saying. Our young man at Gila's lecture could have said: she is a recognized teacher, she writes books on the subject. If she was totally illogical, no one would listen to her. The same goes when you talk with a recognized career counselor or marriage counselor.

Opening your mind to a different view is one of the reasons that people need to seek for themselves a teacher who they go to for their life questions (Way #10 – "Seeking Wisdom from the Wise"). When you have learned important wisdom from someone, it is harder to say that what he is saying to you now is totally wrong and worthless.

Certainly, when you are dealing with the Sages, the wise men of the Jewish people, don't be quick to discount what they say. Don't say, "In those ancient days they just didn't understand human psychology," or "they were prejudiced against women."

The Rabbis say: "A person doesn't really understand the depth of what his teacher is saying until 40 years." What you think you understand now may be wrong.

We need to give special consideration to someone who has demonstrated wisdom. But even an ordinary person deserves some consideration if he says something you totally disagree with. The Rabbis say: "Who is wise? The one who learns from everyone." Everyone has some connection to truth, and maybe what he or she sees is the thing that your emotions block you from seeing. Make an effort to think out *why* they are saying what they are saying. If necessary, play devil's advocate with yourself. Ask your mind for five reasons they could be right, even if you are sure they are wrong.

Another aspect of this Way is to learn how to respectfully argue with your teacher in defense of what you believe. Don't just turn off to what he says, but don't blindly accept it either. If you are convinced of your position, dispute it with him and try to make him wiser. Show him where he is making a mistake. Often you will find that he is really right when he answers your objections. And if it turns out that you were right, then both of you will have a deeper understanding than when you started.

Ways 49 *and* 50

The obvious question, before we start, is: why is there a #49 and #50 of the 48 Ways?

There isn't one accepted explanation. In the eras before printing, texts of Torah were passed down as hand-written documents, from one scribe to the other. If a scribe added his own explanation to a particular Way, it could potentially be copied by the next scribe, and the next one. Once it became part of the text, later copiers wouldn't know that it was an addition, rather than one of the Ways. Rabbi Weinberg believed that this might have happened with Way #5 – "Awe," and Way #6 – "Fear," since awe is a higher level of fear of G-d. Another possibility would be Way #33 – "Loving Doing the Right Things," and Way #34 – "Loving the Straight Path." The straight path is a higher level of doing the right thing.

A more kabbalistic possibility would be based on the fact that there are 50 levels of wisdom, but only G-d has the 50th level. Moshe, the wisest man who ever lived, was on the 49th level. After the 48 Ways, Way #49 tells you how to use all the previous 48 Ways, to take your wisdom to the 49th level. Way #50 – "Saying Something In The Name Of The One Who Said It" – teaches you that all the ideas you have heard in the previous Ways are really from G-d's wisdom, which is the 50th level.

Way · 49

Organizing and Directing your Learning

❡ The Torah is a vast, deep, and complex treasure chest of wisdom. "Its measure is longer than the earth and wider than the sea." To make use of all this information, you need to have tools to organize and retain it so that it is useable when you need it.

❡ Summarize the information you learn and keep it in a way you can easily go back to and review.

❡ Make networks for remembering what you learn. 48 Ways, Pirke Avos, and Chumash parsha-by-parsha are useful networks.

❡ Memorize the networks that are most useful for you.

❡ When you are making decisions in life, review your networks to seek out relevant information.

Way #49, *Mekaven et Sh'muato*, which translates as, "Organizing One's Learning" deals with an issue that is relevant to all the 48 Ways: How do you remember and make use of such a large amount of information? As we have mentioned before, Rabbi Noach Weinberg used to say that when the non-Jewish world discovers the value of even one of the 48 Ways, they make a movement out of it. This was demonstrated earlier with transcendental meditation, neuro-linguistic programming, and the Anthony Robbins fire-walk, which are just taking aspects of Way #9 – "Purity of Mind and Emotion." So how do you keep track of all the powerful ideas contained in the Ways?

This is a problem for anyone who starts being serious with his or her Torah learning. There is so much to remember, and we are constantly learning and forgetting. There are many different forms of Torah – Jewish law, Talmud, philosophical books, Chumash, Tanach, and Midrash, all with important ideas about living on every page. How do we keep it all in our mind, and then access it when confronted with situations in our lives where we need to make use of the Torah's wisdom?

This Way divides the process of holding on to and making use of what you learn, into three parts. First, organize what you learn. Then, work on holding on to it. Lastly, direct and focus what you learn to guide you to the actions you should be taking.

ORGANIZING YOUR LEARNING

To show how this process works, we are going to use the 48 Ways.

The first step to organizing what you learn is to review it, summarize it, and fix it in your mind. Before each Way, I have written a five-statement summary that covers most of the basic ideas of the Way. Reread these summaries to remind yourself. Or reread the Way, and make your own summary. Take those summaries and record them in a book or tablet that you can review periodically.

This method applies to other things you learn, not just 48 Ways. Summarize your learning in your own words in a way you can relate to it, and write down your summaries so you can review them. Once you have them written down, go a step further and have them organized in networks. A network is a set of chapter headings, like the table of contents of a book. Under each chapter, you can put related information.

The 48 Ways is a network for keeping some of the most important ideas about life and personal growth. Each Way is only a few words – "Study," "Listening," "Speaking out" – yet carries with it a connection to many ideas.

Other Judaism networks are the Constant Mitzvot, the Five Levels of Pleasure, the 613 mitzvot, and Pirke Avos. Knowing the Chumash parsha by parsha is another network. The Mishna or the Rambam's Mishne Torah are networks for the information in the Talmud.

A creative person can create his or her own networks. Keep a book with realizations about love and marriage, about business, and about helping the Jewish people.

HOLDING ON TO YOUR LEARNING

Once your learning is organized, you must work to hold on to it. The time-honored way in Judaism to remember your learning was to memorize it. The Sages and their disciples knew all the Chumash and Tanach by heart, as well as the vast amount of information that was later written down in the Talmud.

Today, we do not have the ability or level of commitment to do that. But at least we can think of memorizing a network like the 48 Ways. Memorize the 50 short terms, the titles for each of the Ways that make up the network, and review it often. You will have some of the most powerful ideas about life at your fingertips.

Networks and information we don't memorize can still be reviewed frequently. We read through the Chumash every year in the synagogue. We can review Pirke Avos, which is in every prayer book, in the six weeks between Pesach and Shavuot. Many in the Jewish world are part of the Daf Yomi, a program to finish the Talmud by doing a page a day for seven years, then repeat.

DIRECTING YOUR LEARNING

The purpose of all of this is to use your learning when you need it. For instance, if I want to make a time to think over the purpose of my life, I can go through my networks. Using the 48 Ways, what information do I have for answering the question?

From Way #2 – "Listening" – I can learn to ask the question "What:" "What am I living for?"

From Way #4 – "Understanding of the Heart" – I can ask myself: "What goal do I have that motivates me the most?"

From Way #7 – "Humility" – I can ask: "Am I committed to a cause that takes me out of myself?"

From Way #10 – "Serving Wise Men" – I can ask: "What would my teacher say I should be living for?"

From Way #23 – "Having a Good Heart" – Every human being will die to be good, I can ask myself: "What would I die for, and how do I live for it?"

From Way #31 – "Loving 'the Place'" – Loving G-d is the greatest pleasure, it must be what we are created for. What am I doing to connect myself with it?

In reality, all the 48 Ways can be used to cast light on that important question.

If I want to think out how to help my teenager develop, or my friend deal with his problems, I can look at the 48 Ways on working with people, Ways #39–42. If I want to improve my own learning, I can look at #1 of the 48 Ways – Constant Study, and the learning techniques of Ways #43–#49.

LEARNING TORAH FOR THE SAKE OF G-D

My teacher, Rabbi Noach Weinberg, taught that learning the Torah in order to know and fulfill G-d's instructions for living was "learning for the sake of G-d." That can only be done if we make use of this Way to organize our Torah learning, remember it and use it. If we do this, we are promised the greatest benefits in the world.

Rabbi Meir (in the same chapter of Rabbinic teachings that contains the 48 Ways) said: "Whoever learns Torah for the sake of G-d merits many things; furthermore, the entire world is worthwhile for his sake alone. He is called 'friend,' 'beloved.' He loves the Omnipresent, he loves His creatures, he gladdens the Omnipresent, he gladdens His creatures. His Torah clothes him in humility and fear of G-d; it makes him fit to be righteous, devout, fair and faithful. It moves him away from sin and draws him near to merit. From him people enjoy counsel and wisdom, understanding and strength. . . . The Torah gives him kingship and dominion and analytical judgment; the secrets of the Torah are revealed to him; he becomes like a steadily strengthening fountain and like an unceasing river. He becomes modest, patient, and forgiving of insult to himself. The Torah makes him great and exalts him above all things."

May we all be able to use our Torah and access the power and blessings that come from learning for the sake of G-d.

Way · 50

Giving Credit for your Wisdom (and Bringing the Redemption)

§ The Torah wisdom that we have didn't come from us. It came to us from other wise individuals who in turn received it from previous wise people.

§ All of our wisdom comes from the Almighty, the source of all wisdom.

§ Since that wisdom did not come from us, we shouldn't take credit for it or seek honor from others for it.

§ When we repeat the wisdom we have received, we should say it over in the name of the one we received it from.

§ Wisdom about life is the most valuable gift we can receive. We should be grateful for that gift, and show gratitude to the ones who gave us that gift.

The last of the 48 Ways is *Omer Davar B'shem Omro*, "Saying Something in the Name of the One Who Said it." The Sages meant: don't take credit for the wisdom you are teaching. Let people know from where you received your wisdom. That is why, in the Talmud, it often lists rabbinical statements as Rav X said in the name of Rav Y who said in the name of Rav Z, often listing three or even four people.

Why is that so important?

DON'T TAKE CREDIT FOR YOUR WISDOM

To start, let's ask the question: whose wisdom have you been learning in this book?

Certainly, it's not mine. I've taken Rav Noach Weinberg's wisdom on the 48 Ways, which I heard from him as a yeshiva student more than 40 years ago, and worked with it. When Rav Noach was alive, I was able to get clarification from him on certain points. I taught it over to others for many years, and learned from their feedback. In this book, I have condensed some of it, reorganized some of it, and added some material from my own later learning, life experiences and teaching experience to help in understanding Rav Noach. But I didn't invent any of it. It is from him, not from me.

And where did he get it from? As the foundation for his class, he used a statement of the Sages that the Torah is acquired by 48 Ways. It was his genius that he was able to take this list of 48 short topics and develop them, using his Torah knowledge. But what he demonstrated with his genius was that the comprehensive view of Judaism that comes from his 48 Ways class was already contained in the Sages' concise list. So it wasn't from him, it was from them.

And where did they get it from? They were the inheritors of a tradition that goes back, as traced by Pirke Avos, from the Sages to the Prophets to the Elders to Joshua to Moshe. Each generation added some clarifications and understanding to the principles that Moshe gave them. But their wisdom didn't start from them, it came from Moshe.

And where did Moshe get it from? From the Almighty on Sinai.

We don't own any of our wisdom. It belongs to G-d, the Source of all wisdom.

Since we don't own our wisdom, we shouldn't take credit for it.

It isn't easy to refrain from taking credit for the wisdom we have. We all want to feel that we are smart and insightful. The same drive for respect from others that leads us to seek honor from them for our other virtues leads us to seek honor from them for our wisdom.

But this seeking of honor is not good for us. When you take credit for wisdom that is not your own, it has three negative results:

First, it gives you a wrong perception of yourself. By taking credit, you think that you came up with your ideas because of your own intrinsic genius. You become arrogant, and think you know more than other people, and that you don't have to take what they say seriously.

Second, it causes you to hold on to your ideas even when they are wrong. When you take credit for an idea, you think the one who disagrees with it is personally attacking your intelligence and perceptiveness. If you know that the idea was someone else's idea, it is easier to recognize a better idea when you hear it.

Third, when you take credit, you block yourself from receiving more wisdom. The Almighty, the real source of wisdom, won't send you more, because it will only make you a more arrogant person.

GIVE CREDIT WHERE CREDIT IS DUE

Instead of taking credit for the wisdom you have received, recognize you received it from someone and go out of your way to give credit to the one who taught it to you.

Don't say, "I knew it all along." A really good teacher will show you that you really did know it all along, because the angel taught it to you. But he connected you with it. Say to yourself: *Now* I know that I knew it.

Whenever you hear some useful wisdom on life issues, say to yourself "I am being taught this." It will help you appreciate that what you are being taught is valuable.

When you use these ideas, or teach them to others, give credit to the one who taught you. Say "I learned this from so-and-so."

TREAT WISDOM AS A GIFT

The most important reason for doing this is to recognize that the wisdom you received was a gift. To know what happiness is and how to get it, to know what love is and how to love your spouse better, to know that you can take pleasure in doing good and that pain doesn't destroy pleasure are life lessons that are far more valuable than any gift of money.

Have gratitude for those gifts. We have a mitzvah to be grateful to our parents for giving us life. We need to be grateful to the person who gives us a job or a financial gift. All the more so we need to be grateful to the person who gives us wisdom. Mentioning his name when you use or speak over his wisdom keeps you aware of the debt of gratitude you owe him.

Being grateful to the individual who taught you wisdom teaches you to be grateful to G-d, the true source of all our wisdom.

BRINGING THE WORLD TO REDEMPTION

This Way is the last of the 48 Ways. The Sages ended with a statement reflecting the power of this Way, or perhaps of all the 48 Ways. They said: "Behold, you have learned: Whoever repeats a thing in the name of the one who said it brings redemption to the world, as it is said: 'And Esther said to the King in the name of Mordechai.'"

In the Megillah, Mordechai overhears two of King Ahashverosh's servants plotting against the King. He tells Queen Esther, who tells it to the King. The King has the plotters executed. Esther said that she heard the information from Mordechai, rather than presenting it as her own information, even though it would have gotten her more reward from the King, her husband. Because she said it over in the name of Mordechai, it was put down that way in the chronicles of Persia. The King would be reminded years later of what Mordechai did for him. It would set in motion the series of events that led to the redemption of the Jewish people from the decree of extermination promulgated against them by Haman. Had Esther taken credit for Mordechai's information, Jewish history might have been different.

I can think of two possible explanations for what the Sages wanted to teach us through this example. When we are arrogant, and take credit, we block G-d from sending wisdom to us. Esther, by not taking credit for what she was told, made it possible for G-d to carry out His plan through her. Had she not told the information over in the name of Mordechai, the redemption would have had to take place in another, and perhaps inferior, way.

The Sages could be telling us that, if we don't stand in G-d's path by taking credit for our wisdom, He can send us the wisdom we need to bring about the redemption.

Another explanation would be: what Esther did was not such a difficult thing. She was a great and spiritual woman. She could not have been looking for financial reward or more respect and attention from her husband, the evil King Ahashverosh. By giving credit to Mordechai, she fulfilled this 48 Way by doing something that was easy to do. Yet it still brought redemption to the world.

What if we did something even harder than what she did? Could we bring redemption to the world? The Rabbis could be saying: Imagine if we fulfilled a 48 Way that was even more difficult for us to do! Imagine we did all the 48 Ways! Imagine it wasn't just one person but many of us!

May our continuing with the 48 Ways and using the great wisdom of Rabbi Noach Weinberg, which is the wisdom of the Sages, which is the wisdom of the Almighty, bring us the redemption that we so badly need and long for, in this generation.

Notes

Way #1 | Life-Long Study
"It isn't upon you to finish the work." Pirke Avos, 2:21
"Longer than the earth, and wider than the sea." Iyov 11:9
Majority of a person's wisdom comes from learning at night. Rambam,
    Hilchot Talmud Torah 3:13

Way #2 | Listening to Life's Messages
"The world was created for me." Mishna Sanhedrin 4:5
Story of Rabbi Yehoshua ben Levi and Eliyahu. Sanhedrin 98a

Way #3 | Using the Power of Speech
The Rabbis say: "Always teach your students in a minimum of words."
    Pesachim 3b

**Way #4 | Connecting with Your Intuition: Understanding of the
        Heart**
Story of the angel. Nida 30b
When he repeats it, it becomes permissible. Sota 22a
David cutting the garment of Shaul. Shmuel I, 24:6–7, with Malbim

Way #5 | the Power of Awe
"When I see the heavens the work of your hands . . . what is man that
    you should remember him." Tehillim 8:4–5

Way #6 | Embracing Fear
"Everything is in the hands of G-d except fear of G-d." Berachot 33b
"Do not be scornful of any person." Pirke Avos 4:3
"If Israel does *teshuva*" Rabbi Eliezer, Sanhedrin 97b

Way #7 | Living with Humility
Moshe, "The humblest man." Bamidbar 12:3

Way #8 | Living with Joy
"The reason for the exile was because we didn't serve G-d with joy . . ."
    Devarim 28:47–48
"Prophecy only rests on a person who has joy." Rambam, Hilchot Yesodei
    Hatorah 7:4

Way #9 | Purity of Mind and Emotion
"I keep G-d in front of me always." Tehillim 16:8
"Look deeply at 3 things. . . ." Pirke Avos 2:1
"What is the love of G-d that is fitting?" Rambam, Hilchot Teshuva 10:3
"All your actions should be for the sake of G-d." Pirke Avos 2:17
"The foundation of all wisdoms. . . ." Rav Moshe Chaim Luzzatto,
    Mesilat Yesharim, Chapter 1

Way #10 | Seeking Wisdom from the Wise
"Who is the wise man?" Pirke Avos 4:1
Stand for an elderly non-Jew. Kiddushin 33a
"Make for yourself a teacher." Pirke Avos 1:6
"Even if he is smaller in wisdom than you . . ." Rambam, commentary on
    Avos
"A person should always live in the place of his teacher." Berachot 8a

Way #11 | Having a Real Friend
"Buy yourself a friend." Pirke Avos 1:6

Way #12 | Growth through Teaching: The Questioning of Students
"It is a mitzvah on every wise man." Rambam, Hilchot Talmud Torah, 1:2
"I learned a lot from my teachers." Taanit 7a
"Stand up many students." Pirke Avos 1:1

Way #13 | Searching your Mind for Wisdom with Deliberateness
"Be deliberate in judgment." Pirke Avos 1:1
The #1 goal of the *yetzer hara*. Rabbi Moshe Chaim Luzzatto, Mesilat
    Yesharim, Ch 2
Rav Elazar ben Arach, "an ever-flowing spring of water." Pirke Avos 2:11
"Be diligent in the study of Torah." Pirke Avos 2:19

Way #16 | Minimize Business (But Learn from it also)
"If you seek it like money. . . ." Proverbs 2:4–5
"Calculate the loss from a mitzvah compared to its reward." Pirke Avos,
   2:1
"Limit your work, and work in Torah." Pirke Avos 4:12

Way #17 | Minimize *Derech Eretz* (But Learn from it also)
Shir Hashirim is "the holy of holies." Mishna Yadayim 3:5
"I am sick with love." Shir Hashirim 5:8

Way #18 | Minimize Physical Pleasure (But Learn from it also)
"All your actions should be for the sake of Heaven." Pirke Avos 2:17

Way #19 | Minimize Sleep (But Learn from it also)
"Sleep is 1/60th of death." Berachot 57b
The *shofar* is a wake-up call. Rambam Hilchot Teshuva, 3:4

Way #22 | Conquering Anger and Frustration
"Life of an angry man is not a life." Pesachim 113b
"As if he is worshipping idols." Shabbat 105b
"All easy ways need to be examined." Mesilat Yesharim, Ch 6
"A righteous person falls 7 times and gets up." Proverbs 24:16
The story of Rabbi Akiva and the stone. Avos of Rebbe Nasan 6:2

Way #23 | Being a Good Person: Having a Good Heart
"I have placed before you today the life and the good, the death and the
   evil. . . . Choose life." Devarim 30:15–19
The righteous person is considered alive even after his death, whereas the
   wicked are considered dead even when they are alive. Berachot 18a–18b
The martyrdom of Rabbi Akiva. Berachot 61b

Way #24 | Belief in Wise People
Elisha and Eliyahu. Kings I, 19:19–21
"Who poured water on the hands of Eliyahu." Kings II, 3:11

Way #25 | Enduring and Accepting Pain
"When you have a headache, study Torah." Eruvin 54a
"According to the pain is the reward." Pirke Avos 5:21
"Like a father chastises a son, so does G-d chastise you." Devarim 8:5

Way #26 | Knowing Your Place in the World
Court of 23 seated "according to their level of wisdom," Rambam,
    Hilchot Sanhedrin 1:7
"The world was created for me." Mishna Sanhedrin 4:5
"If I am not for myself, who will be for me?" Pirke Avos 1:14
"Envy, desire, and honor take a man out of the world." Pirke Avos 4:28
"Don't be a wicked person in your own eyes." Pirke Avos 2:18
"He looked this way and that, and saw there was no man." Shmot 2:12
Yeravam – who will go first? Sanhedrin 102a

Way #27 | The Pathway to Happiness: Being Happy with One's
                 Portion
"Who is rich?" Pirke Avos, 4:1

Way #28 | Being a Realist: Making a Fence for Our Life Goals
"Make a fence for the Torah." Pirke Avos 1:1
"Our biggest mistake," Rabbi Luzzatto, Path of the Just, Chapter 2
"Three crowns," Pirke Avos 4:17
"Better to be a tail to lions than the head of a group of foxes." Pirke Avos
    4:20
"Who is wise? The one who sees what will come." Tamid 32a

Way #29 | Taking Pleasure, Not Credit
Rabbi Yochanan ben Zakkai, "if you have learned a lot of Torah . . ."
    Pirke Avos 2:9
"Man was only created to take pleasure in G-d." Mesilat Yesharim Ch. 1
Eliezer bows when he hears good news, Bereishit 24:26 and 24:52
"The power and strength of my hand" Devarim 8:17
Hillel: "the one who builds up his name, loses his name." Pirke Avos 1:13
Nebuchadnezzar losing his power, Book of Daniel 4:27–29

Way #30 | Love Yourself
"Don't be a wicked person in your own eyes." Pirke Avos 2:18

Way #31 | Love the Transcendental
"A person should love G-d. . . ." Rambam Hilchot Teshuva 10:3
"To love G-d, make him loved by the creations." Rambam Sefer
    Hamitzvot Positive Mitzvah #3
"When a person thinks about G-d's actions and His wondrous creations."
    Rambam Hilchot Yesodei Hatorah, 2:2

Way #34 | Love the Straight Path

"G-d created man straight, but they sought many rationalizations".
Koheles 7:29

"What is the straight way that a man should choose? Whatever is beautiful to himself. . . ." Pirke Avos 2:1

Way #35 | Love Accepting and Giving Criticism

"Judge everyone to the side of merit." Pirke Avos 1:6

G-d and the attribute of justice, Shabbat 54b

Way #36 | Distance Yourself from Honor

"Who is the wise man?" Pirke Avos 4:1

"Good to Great." Jim Collins

Way #37 | Making Everything New: Not Becoming Complacent in his Studies

"Don't despise any person." Pirke Avos 4:3

"There are those who acquire their World-to-Come in one hour." Avoda Zara 17a

Way #38 | The Seriousness of Giving Advice: Not Taking Joy in Teaching Others What To Do

"Teach your tongue to say 'I don't know.'" Berachot 4a

Way #39 | Caring for People: Sharing the Burden with your Fellow Man

"The world was created for me." Mishna Sanhedrin 4:5

"Love the stranger like yourself, for you were strangers in the land of Egypt." Vayikra 19:34

Moshe in Egypt, "He saw their burdens." Shmot 2:11

Way #41 | Giving Inner Clarity: Standing on Truth

Story of Onkelos. Avoda Zara 11a

Way #42 | Giving Inner Peace

Hitler, from *Inside the Third Reich*, Albert Speer

Mao, from *Mao, The Unknown Story*, Jung Chang & Jon Halliday

Abraham, test of *Lech Lecha* 12:1–2, with Rashi; test of *Akeida* 22:1–3

Way #43 | Desiring to Learn

Kohen Gadol on Yom Kippur night, Mishna Yoma, 1:6

Notes

"Always a person should learn what his heart desires." Avoda Zara 19a

Way #45 | The Key to Creativity: Hearing and Adding On
"Love work" Pirke Avos 1:10

Way #47 | Bringing Learning into the Real World: Learning in Order to Do
"If not now, when?" Pirke Avos 1:14

Way #48 | Fighting a Closed Mind: Making One's Teacher Wise
You don't understand your teacher until 40 years. Devarim 29:3, Rashi on Pirke Avos 5:22
"Who is wise?" Pirke Avos 4:1

Way #49 | Organizing and Directing One's Learning
"Its measure is longer than the earth." Job 11:9
Rabbi Meir: "Anyone who learns Torah for the sake of G-d ..." Masechta Kallah Rabbati
This chapter is normally printed in *siddurim* as the sixth chapter of Pirke Avos 6:1